Ransomware Defense Strategies

Proven Defense Strategies for Today's
Threat Landscape

Jack Taylor

Welcome to "Ransomware Defense Strategies - Proven Defense Strategies for Today's Threat Landscape." I'm thrilled to embark on this journey with you as we explore the world of ransomware and arm ourselves with effective defense strategies.

As a cybersecurity professional with years of experience in battling ransomware attacks, I've witnessed firsthand the devastating impact these malicious acts can have on organizations and individuals. The ever-evolving threat landscape demands a proactive approach to safeguard our digital assets, and that's precisely what this book aims to deliver.

In this book, we will delve into the intricate workings of ransomware attacks, understanding the anatomy of these insidious threats. From the initial infiltration to the encryption of critical data and the daunting ransom demands, we will dissect the attack process and equip ourselves with the knowledge needed to thwart these malicious attempts.

But it doesn't stop there. Prevention is undoubtedly essential, and we will explore how to assess your security posture to identify vulnerabilities and weaknesses. We will discuss building a resilient infrastructure, fortifying your networks, implementing robust backup and disaster recovery strategies, and establishing secure configurations and access controls.

Recognizing the pivotal role of human factors in cybersecurity, we will delve into the importance of user awareness and training. Educating employees about ransomware risks, fostering secure practices for email, web browsing, and file sharing, and creating a culture of security within organizations are crucial elements in our defense arsenal.

No matter how well we prepare, the possibility of a ransomware incident remains. That's why we will delve into incident response and recovery strategies. From developing an effective incident response plan to containing the attack, mitigating the impact, and recovering encrypted data, we will explore the steps required to restore normalcy in the face of adversity.

To stay one step ahead, we will dive into advanced defense techniques. Utilizing threat intelligence, proactive monitoring, behavior-based detection, and machine learning will bolster our defenses against the ever-changing ransomware landscape. We will also discuss encryption and data protection mechanisms, as well as the implementation of deception technologies to outsmart attackers.

Understanding the power of collaboration, we will emphasize the importance of information sharing. Engaging with industry peers, security communities, and law enforcement agencies allows us to leverage collective knowledge, share threat intelligence, and foster a united front against ransomware attackers.

Compliance with data protection regulations and standards is crucial in today's landscape. We will explore the compliance and regulatory considerations specific to ransomware defense, ensuring that our strategies align with industry-specific security frameworks.

Finally, we will take a glimpse into the future. The world of ransomware continues to evolve, and we must anticipate emerging trends and technologies. We will discuss the potential impact of artificial intelligence, machine learning, quantum computing, and predictive analytics on the ransomware landscape, preparing ourselves for the challenges that lie ahead.

Throughout this book, my aim is to provide you with practical, actionable strategies and insights based on proven methods. By combining technical knowledge, best practices, and real-world examples, we will empower ourselves to defend against ransomware attacks and protect our most valuable assets.

Let's embark on this journey together and arm ourselves with the knowledge and skills needed to defend against ransomware in today's ever-changing threat landscape.

Jack Taylor

Chapter 1: Introduction to Ransomware......................... **9**

1.1 What is Ransomware?... 11

1.2 A Brief History of Ransomware Attacks................ 17

1.3 Ransomware's Impact on Organizations and
Individuals.. 21

Chapter 2: Ransomware Attack Anatomy..................... **25**

2.1 Stages of a Ransomware Attack.......................... 27

2.2 Types of Ransomware: Encrypting, Locker, and
Hybrid..31

2.3 Common Attack Vectors: Phishing, Malvertising,
and Exploit Kits... 34

Chapter 3: Assessing Your Security Posture.............. **38**

3.1 Conducting a Security Risk Assessment.............. 40

3.2 Identifying Vulnerabilities and Weak Points.......... 44

3.3 Evaluating Readiness to Defend Against
Ransomware...48

Chapter 4: Building a Resilient Infrastructure............. **54**

4.1 Implementing Robust Backup Strategies..............57

4.2 Disaster Recovery Planning and Testing.............. 61

4.3 Strengthening Network Security: Firewalls,
Intrusion Detection Systems (IDS), and Intrusion
Prevention Systems (IPS)..65

4.4 Enhancing Endpoint Security: Antivirus, Endpoint
Detection and Response (EDR), and Host-based
Firewalls...71

4.5 Secure Configurations and Access Controls: Patch
Management, Least Privilege, and Network
Segmentation...76

Chapter 5: User Awareness and Training.....................**82**

5.1 Ransomware Education and Awareness Programs.
85

5.2 Best Practices for Email Security........................89

5.3 Safe Web Browsing and Downloading Practices..93

5.4 Secure File Sharing and Collaboration................. 96

Chapter 6: Incident Response and Recovery............ 100

6.1 Developing an Incident Response Plan.............. 103

6.2 Initial Response and Containment Strategies..... 107

6.3 Mitigation and Removal of Ransomware............ 111

6.4 Data Recovery: Backup Restoration and File Decryption... 115

Chapter 7: Advanced Defense Techniques............... 119

7.1 Threat Intelligence and Proactive Monitoring..... 122

7.2 Behavior-Based Detection and Machine Learning... 127

7.3 Endpoint Detection and Response (EDR) Solutions 131

7.4 Data Encryption and Protection Mechanisms..... 135

7.5 Deception Technologies: Honeypots and Honeytokens.. 140

Chapter 8: Collaboration and Information Sharing... 144

8.1 Engaging with Industry Peers and Security Communities... 147

8.2 Sharing Threat Intelligence and Best Practices.. 151

8.3 Collaborating with Law Enforcement and Cybersecurity Organizations..................................... 155

Chapter 9: Compliance and Regulatory Considerations 160

9.1 Overview of Data Protection Regulations and Standards... 163

9.2 Incorporating Compliance Requirements into Ransomware Defense.. 167

9.3 Security Frameworks: NIST Cybersecurity Framework, ISO 27001, etc...................................... 171

Chapter 10: Future Trends and Emerging Technologies 177

10.1 Evolving Landscape of Ransomware Attacks: Ransomware-as-a-Service (RaaS), AI-driven attacks, etc.. 180

10.2 Role of Artificial Intelligence and Machine
Learning in Ransomware Defense............................ 184

10.3 Predictive Analytics and Threat Hunting........... 188

10.4 Quantum Computing and Its Potential Impact on
Ransomware..191

Chapter 1: Introduction to Ransomware

Welcome to the world of ransomware, where digital extortion has become an all too common threat. In this chapter, we will embark on a journey to understand the fundamentals of ransomware and its profound impact on organizations and individuals alike.

Section 1.1: What is Ransomware?

To navigate the realm of ransomware effectively, we must first grasp its essence. In this section, we will explore the definition of ransomware, uncovering its core characteristics and how it differentiates itself from other forms of malware. By understanding the inner workings of ransomware, we lay the foundation for developing effective defense strategies.

Section 1.2: A Brief History of Ransomware Attacks

Ransomware is not a new phenomenon. In this section, we will delve into the historical context of ransomware attacks, tracing its origins and evolution over time. By examining notable cases and prominent attack vectors from the past, we gain valuable insights into the tactics employed by cybercriminals and the lessons learned from previous incidents.

Section 1.3: Ransomware's Impact on Organizations and Individuals

The consequences of falling victim to a ransomware attack can be catastrophic. In this section, we explore the profound impact of ransomware on organizations and individuals. We examine the financial losses, operational disruptions, reputational damage, and emotional toll that victims endure. By understanding the gravity of these attacks, we strengthen our resolve to proactively defend against them.

Ransomware poses a significant threat in today's digital landscape, and it's imperative that we arm ourselves with knowledge and strategies to mitigate this risk. This chapter has laid the groundwork for our exploration of ransomware, providing a solid understanding of its definition, historical context, and the wide-ranging impact it can have. Armed with this knowledge, we are prepared to dive deeper into the intricacies of ransomware defense strategies in the chapters that follow.

Together, let's unravel the complexities of ransomware and equip ourselves with the tools and insights needed to protect our digital assets from this pervasive threat.

1.1 What is Ransomware?

Ransomware is a malicious software that encrypts the victim's files or locks their computer, rendering the data inaccessible. The attacker then demands a ransom, usually in the form of cryptocurrency, in exchange for the decryption key or the release of the compromised system. Ransomware attacks have become a significant cybersecurity threat, targeting individuals, businesses, and even government organizations.

1.1.1 Evolution of Ransomware

Ransomware has evolved significantly since its inception in the late 1980s. The early versions, known as "scareware," used social engineering tactics to trick victims into paying for fake security software. However, modern ransomware has become more sophisticated, employing advanced encryption algorithms and leveraging various attack vectors.

The emergence of cryptocurrencies, such as Bitcoin, played a significant role in the proliferation of ransomware. Cryptocurrencies provide an anonymous and decentralized method of receiving ransom payments, making it difficult to trace the attackers. This development led to the rise of ransomware-as-a-service (RaaS) models, where cybercriminals provide ransomware tools and infrastructure to other attackers in exchange for a percentage of the profits.

1.1.2 Ransomware Attack Lifecycle

Understanding the stages of a ransomware attack can help organizations develop effective defense strategies. The typical ransomware attack follows a lifecycle that involves the following stages:

1.1.2.1. Delivery: Ransomware is usually delivered through various means, such as malicious email attachments, exploit kits, malicious websites, or compromised software updates. Attackers often employ social engineering techniques to trick victims into opening infected files or clicking on malicious links.

1.1.2.2. Execution: Once the ransomware gains access to a system, it executes its payload, which can involve encrypting files, modifying system settings, or deploying additional malware. The encryption process often targets a wide range of file types, including documents, images, databases, and backups, making them inaccessible to the victim.

1.1.2.3. Encryption: The encryption stage uses strong cryptographic algorithms to lock the victim's files, rendering them unreadable without the decryption key. The key is typically held by the attacker, who demands a ransom to provide it.

1.1.2.4. Ransom Note: After the encryption process is complete, the attacker leaves a ransom note, either as a text file or a pop-up message, informing the victim about the attack and providing instructions on how to pay the ransom. The note may include threats of permanent data loss or increased ransom demands if the payment is not made within a specified timeframe.

1.1.2.5. Ransom Payment: To receive the decryption key, the victim is instructed to pay the ransom, often in a cryptocurrency like Bitcoin. The payment process is designed to be anonymous and untraceable, making it challenging for law enforcement agencies to track down the attackers.

1.1.2.6. Decryption: If the victim decides to pay the ransom, they may receive the decryption key to unlock their files. However, there is no guarantee that the attacker will fulfill their end of the bargain, as some attackers may simply take the payment and disappear without providing the necessary decryption key.

1.1.3 Impact and Consequences

Ransomware attacks can have severe consequences for individuals and organizations alike. The impact of a successful ransomware attack can include:

1.1.3.1. Data Loss: The encryption process of ransomware can lead to permanent data loss if victims do not have proper backups or cannot obtain the decryption key.

1.1.3.2. Financial Loss: Organizations may incur significant financial losses due to ransom payments, downtime, and the costs associated with incident response, investigation, and recovery efforts.

1.1.3.3. Reputation Damage: Publicized ransomware attacks can damage the reputation and trustworthiness of organizations, resulting in customer and partner loss.

1.1.3.4. Operational Disruption: Ransomware attacks can cause significant disruptions to business operations, leading to productivity losses and potential service outages.

1.1.3.5. Legal and Regulatory Consequences: In some cases, organizations may face legal and regulatory consequences if they fail to protect sensitive data or adequately respond to a ransomware incident, resulting in potential fines or lawsuits.

1.1.4 Defense Strategies and Prevention

Preventing and mitigating the impact of ransomware attacks requires a multi-layered approach to cybersecurity. Organizations can implement the following defense strategies:

1.1.4.1. Regular Backups: Maintain up-to-date backups of critical data in offline or remote locations to ensure data can be restored in case of a ransomware attack.

1.1.4.2. Security Awareness Training: Educate employees about the risks of phishing emails, suspicious attachments, and unsafe browsing habits. Encourage a security-conscious culture within the organization.

1.1.4.3. Patch and Update Management: Regularly apply security patches and updates to operating systems, software, and applications to address known vulnerabilities that attackers often exploit.

1.1.4.4. Robust Endpoint Protection: Deploy and regularly update anti-malware and endpoint protection solutions to detect and block ransomware threats.

1.1.4.5. Network Segmentation: Implement network segmentation to restrict lateral movement of ransomware within the network, limiting the potential impact of an attack.

1.1.4.6. Incident Response Planning: Develop an incident response plan that outlines the steps to be taken in the event of a ransomware attack, including communication protocols, isolation of infected systems, and recovery procedures.

1.1.4.7. Threat Intelligence Sharing: Collaborate with industry peers, government agencies, and security vendors to share threat intelligence and stay updated on the latest ransomware trends and attack techniques.

Ransomware poses a significant threat to individuals and organizations, causing financial losses, data breaches, and operational disruptions. Understanding the nature of ransomware, its attack lifecycle, and the potential consequences is crucial for developing effective defense strategies.

By implementing proactive measures, such as regular backups, employee training, patch management, and robust endpoint protection, organizations can enhance their resilience against ransomware attacks. Furthermore, staying informed about emerging ransomware trends and technologies can help organizations adapt their defenses to the evolving threat landscape.

As ransomware continues to evolve, organizations must remain vigilant, adopt a comprehensive approach to cybersecurity, and invest in technologies and practices that safeguard their valuable data and systems.

1.2 A Brief History of Ransomware Attacks

Ransomware attacks have a long history dating back to the late 1980s. Over the years, these malicious campaigns have evolved in complexity, tactics, and targets. Understanding the historical context of ransomware can provide valuable insights into the progression of this cyber threat and the motivations behind it.

1.2.1 The Emergence of Ransomware

The first known instance of ransomware, known as the "AIDS Trojan," appeared in 1989. This ransomware was distributed via floppy disks and targeted healthcare professionals, claiming to provide information about AIDS research. However, upon execution, it encrypted files on the victim's hard drive and demanded a payment to a specified address to decrypt them. The payment method involved sending physical mail to a post office box.

1.2.2 Encryption-Based Ransomware

In the early 2000s, encryption-based ransomware started to gain traction. The "GPCode" ransomware, discovered in 2004, used strong RSA encryption to lock victims' files. It demanded a ransom in exchange for the decryption key. Although early versions of encryption-based ransomware were often poorly implemented and could be decrypted without paying the ransom, attackers soon improved their encryption algorithms, making decryption without the key virtually impossible.

1.2.3 Police-themed Ransomware

Around 2010, a new variant of ransomware known as "police-themed ransomware" emerged. These attacks typically displayed a fake law enforcement message claiming that the victim had committed illegal activities, such as distributing child pornography or engaging in copyright infringement. The ransomware demanded a fine payment to unlock the victim's computer and avoid legal consequences. These attacks often exploited social engineering tactics to deceive victims into believing the messages were legitimate.

1.2.4 CryptoLocker and the Rise of Ransomware-as-a-Service (RaaS)

In 2013, the CryptoLocker ransomware gained notoriety for its sophisticated encryption capabilities and effective distribution methods. CryptoLocker employed robust encryption algorithms, making file decryption extremely difficult without the attacker's private key. It was also one of the first notable instances of ransomware employing a Bitcoin payment system, which provided attackers with an anonymous and untraceable method of receiving ransom payments.

CryptoLocker's success paved the way for the rise of ransomware-as-a-service (RaaS) models. RaaS allows cybercriminals to rent or purchase ransomware kits from developers, who earn a percentage of the profits generated by the attacks. This approach made ransomware more accessible to a wider range of attackers, contributing to the proliferation of ransomware campaigns.

1.2.5 Targeting Enterprises and Critical Infrastructure

In recent years, ransomware attacks have increasingly targeted businesses and critical infrastructure. Attackers recognized the potential for higher ransom payments by encrypting sensitive corporate data or disrupting essential services. Notable attacks include the 2017 "WannaCry" and "NotPetya" outbreaks, which affected organizations globally, including healthcare systems, government agencies, and major corporations. These attacks highlighted the devastating impact ransomware can have on critical operations and the need for robust defenses.

1.2.6 Evolution of Ransomware Tactics

As defenders improved their ransomware detection and mitigation techniques, attackers adapted their tactics to maximize their success rates. This led to the emergence of new tactics, such as "double extortion," where attackers not only encrypt files but also threaten to release stolen data if the ransom is not paid. This tactic adds another layer of pressure on victims, increasing the likelihood of payment.

Furthermore, attackers have increasingly focused on exploiting vulnerabilities in remote desktop protocols (RDP), compromising unpatched systems, and targeting specific industries or organizations with higher financial resources.

The history of ransomware attacks demonstrates their evolution from simple scams to sophisticated, high-stakes cyber threats. From early encryption-based attacks to the emergence of police-themed ransomware and the rise of RaaS models, ransomware campaigns have continuously adapted to maximize profits and exploit vulnerabilities.

Understanding the historical context of ransomware provides valuable insights into the motivations and tactics of attackers. It also underscores the importance of robust cybersecurity practices, such as regular software updates, employee education, and proactive defense measures, to protect against these evolving threats. As ransomware continues to evolve, organizations must remain vigilant, stay informed about emerging trends, and implement effective strategies to mitigate the risk of attacks.

1.3 Ransomware's Impact on Organizations and Individuals

Ransomware attacks have become a significant and costly cybersecurity threat, impacting both organizations and individuals worldwide. The consequences of a successful ransomware attack can be far-reaching, affecting not only financial and operational aspects but also the privacy and trust of those targeted.

1.3.1 Financial Losses

Ransomware attacks can result in substantial financial losses for organizations. The ransom demanded by attackers can range from a few hundred dollars to millions, depending on the target's perceived value and ability to pay. Moreover, the costs associated with incident response, investigation, system restoration, and potential legal actions can quickly escalate. These expenses include engaging cybersecurity experts, conducting forensic analysis, implementing enhanced security measures, and recovering compromised data.

1.3.2 Operational Disruptions

Ransomware attacks can cause severe operational disruptions for organizations. When critical systems and files are encrypted or inaccessible, businesses may experience significant downtime, affecting productivity, customer service, and revenue generation. Operational disruptions can also result in reputational damage, customer dissatisfaction, and the loss of business opportunities.

1.3.3 Data Loss and Privacy Breaches

One of the primary objectives of ransomware attacks is to encrypt or compromise valuable data. In some cases, victims may lose access to their data permanently if they cannot restore it from secure backups or decrypt it using the attacker-provided key. The loss of sensitive information can have severe implications, including violation of data protection regulations, breach of customer trust, and potential legal consequences.

Additionally, ransomware attacks may involve exfiltrating data before encryption and threatening its public release if the ransom is not paid. This double extortion tactic further compromises privacy and exposes organizations to potential data breaches and reputational damage.

1.3.4 Reputational Damage and Trust Issues

Publicly disclosed ransomware attacks can significantly impact an organization's reputation and erode customer trust. News of a successful attack can damage the perception of an organization's security posture, potentially leading to a loss of customers, partners, and investors. Organizations may face challenges in rebuilding trust and assuring stakeholders that their data will be protected in the future.

1.3.5 Legal and Regulatory Consequences

Ransomware attacks can have legal and regulatory ramifications for organizations. Depending on the jurisdiction and industry-specific regulations, organizations may be obligated to report data breaches and take appropriate measures to safeguard personal information. Failure to meet these obligations can result in regulatory fines, legal liabilities, and lawsuits from affected individuals or regulatory authorities.

1.3.6 Psychological Impact on Individuals

Ransomware attacks can also have a significant psychological impact on individuals, particularly if personal data or sensitive information is compromised. Victims may experience feelings of violation, anxiety, and helplessness. This emotional toll can extend to employees within organizations, leading to decreased morale, job dissatisfaction, and increased stress levels.

Ransomware attacks have profound implications for both organizations and individuals. The financial losses, operational disruptions, data loss, reputational damage, and trust issues associated with these attacks can have long-lasting consequences. Organizations must prioritize robust cybersecurity measures, including proactive defenses, employee education, regular backups, and incident response planning, to mitigate the risk of ransomware attacks and minimize their impact. Additionally, individuals should remain vigilant, exercise caution when interacting with suspicious emails or websites, and stay informed about the evolving threat landscape. By taking these proactive steps, organizations and individuals can better protect themselves against the growing menace of ransomware.

Chapter 2: Ransomware Attack Anatomy

In the realm of cybersecurity, knowledge is power. To effectively defend against ransomware attacks, we must understand their inner workings. In this chapter, we will dissect the anatomy of ransomware attacks, exploring the various stages, types of ransomware, and common attack vectors employed by cybercriminals. By unraveling the intricacies of ransomware attack anatomy, we empower ourselves with the insights needed to develop robust defense strategies.

Section 2.1: Stages of a Ransomware Attack

Ransomware attacks follow a well-defined lifecycle, with distinct stages that cybercriminals navigate to accomplish their malicious objectives. In this section, we will explore each stage in detail, from initial infiltration and establishment of persistence to the encryption of critical data and the eventual ransom demand. By understanding the sequential progression of a ransomware attack, we can identify key points of intervention and strengthen our defenses accordingly.

Section 2.2: Types of Ransomware: Encrypting, Locker, and Hybrid

Ransomware comes in various forms, each with its unique characteristics and objectives. In this section, we will examine the different types of ransomware, including encrypting ransomware, locker ransomware, and hybrid variants. By understanding the distinctions between these types, we can tailor our defense strategies to effectively combat the specific ransomware threats we may encounter.

Section 2.3: Common Attack Vectors

The success of a ransomware attack often relies on exploiting vulnerabilities in systems and human behaviors. In this section, we will explore the most common attack vectors used by cybercriminals to initiate ransomware infections. From phishing emails and malicious attachments to drive-by downloads and exploit kits, we will examine how attackers exploit these vectors to gain a foothold in their targets' systems. By recognizing these attack vectors, we can implement targeted preventive measures and educate ourselves and our organizations on how to detect and avoid falling victim to them.

Understanding the anatomy of a ransomware attack is paramount in developing effective defense strategies. This chapter has delved into the stages of a ransomware attack, the different types of ransomware, and the common attack vectors used by cybercriminals. Armed with this knowledge, we can better comprehend the modus operandi of attackers and identify vulnerabilities in our systems and practices.

As we proceed in this book, we will build upon this understanding and explore proven defense strategies to counter each stage of a ransomware attack. By dissecting the tactics and techniques employed by ransomware operators, we can fortify our defenses and safeguard our digital assets from this pervasive threat.

Let us now venture further into the world of ransomware defense, equipped with a deeper understanding of its attack anatomy. Together, we will forge resilient defenses and stay one step ahead of those who seek to hold our data hostage.

2.1 Stages of a Ransomware Attack

A ransomware attack typically follows a series of stages, each serving a specific purpose in the attacker's objective to encrypt data and demand a ransom. Understanding these stages can help organizations develop effective defense strategies and response plans to mitigate the impact of such attacks.

2.1.1 Stage 1: Reconnaissance

In the reconnaissance stage, attackers gather information about potential targets. This includes identifying vulnerable systems, exploitable software, and potential entry points into the target network. Attackers may employ various methods such as scanning for open ports, researching target organizations' online presence, or using social engineering techniques to gather intelligence.

2.1.2 Stage 2: Initial Compromise

Once the reconnaissance is complete, attackers initiate the initial compromise of the target network. This can be achieved through various means, such as phishing emails, malicious attachments, exploit kits, or exploiting unpatched software vulnerabilities. By exploiting a vulnerability or tricking a user into executing malicious code, the attacker gains an initial foothold within the network.

2.1.3 Stage 3: Lateral Movement

Once inside the network, attackers seek to expand their access and move laterally across the network to gain control over additional systems. They exploit weak security controls, misconfigured permissions, or compromised user credentials to move from one system to another. This stage allows the attacker to locate valuable data, escalate privileges, and gain control over critical systems.

2.1.4 Stage 4: System Exploitation

At this stage, the attacker identifies and exploits vulnerabilities in the target systems to gain administrative control. They may leverage exploits, deploy custom malware, or use tools that allow them to gain complete control over the compromised systems. Exploiting vulnerabilities allows the attacker to ensure persistence and maintain access to the network even after initial infection vectors are removed.

2.1.5 Stage 5: Encryption and Ransom

Once the attacker has established control over the target systems, they initiate the encryption process. They encrypt files, folders, or even entire systems using strong encryption algorithms, making the data inaccessible without the decryption key. After the encryption is complete, the attacker presents a ransom note, typically in the form of a pop-up message or text file, demanding a payment in exchange for the decryption key. The ransom note often includes instructions on how to make the payment, the amount demanded, and threats of permanent data loss or public data exposure if the ransom is not paid within a specified timeframe.

2.1.6 Stage 6: Payment and Decrypting

If the victim decides to pay the ransom, they typically follow the instructions provided by the attacker, which may involve making a cryptocurrency payment such as Bitcoin. Once the payment is made, the attacker may provide the decryption key or a decryption tool to unlock the encrypted data. However, there is no guarantee that the attacker will uphold their end of the bargain, and there have been instances where victims who paid the ransom did not receive the promised decryption key.

2.1.7 Stage 7: Post-Incident Remediation

After the attack, organizations must undertake a series of remediation efforts. This includes isolating infected systems, removing the ransomware from the network, restoring data from backups, and closing any security gaps that allowed the attack to occur. It is crucial to conduct a thorough investigation to determine the attack's origin, the extent of the damage, and to identify any additional vulnerabilities that could be exploited.

Understanding the stages of a ransomware attack provides valuable insights into the attacker's methodology and can help organizations develop effective defense strategies. By implementing strong security measures, conducting regular security assessments, and educating employees about the risks of phishing and other attack vectors, organizations can better protect themselves against ransomware attacks. Additionally, having an incident response plan in place enables a swift and coordinated response to minimize the impact of an attack and facilitate the recovery process.

2.2 Types of Ransomware: Encrypting, Locker, and Hybrid

Ransomware comes in various forms, each with its own characteristics and techniques. Understanding the different types of ransomware can help organizations develop targeted defense strategies and enhance their ability to detect, prevent, and respond to these threats effectively. The three primary types of ransomware are encrypting ransomware, locker ransomware, and hybrid ransomware.

2.2.1 Encrypting Ransomware

Encrypting ransomware is the most common type of ransomware encountered. It encrypts the victim's files using robust encryption algorithms, rendering them inaccessible without the decryption key. When encrypting ransomware infects a system, it typically targets a wide range of file types, including documents, images, videos, databases, and more. Once the encryption process is complete, the attacker presents the victim with a ransom demand and instructions on how to make the payment to obtain the decryption key.

Encrypting ransomware is designed to maximize the potential financial gain for attackers. The encryption process is often executed using strong and unbreakable encryption algorithms, making it extremely difficult, if not impossible, to decrypt the files without the attacker's key. Examples of well-known encrypting ransomware include CryptoLocker, WannaCry, and Locky.

2.2.2 Locker Ransomware

Locker ransomware, also known as screen-locking ransomware, focuses on denying the victim access to their system or specific functionalities without encrypting their files. This type of ransomware typically displays a full-screen message or locks the user's desktop, preventing them from accessing their operating system or essential applications. The ransom note displayed on the locked screen includes instructions on how to pay the ransom to regain access to the system.

Locker ransomware often targets mobile devices, such as smartphones or tablets, but can also affect desktop or laptop computers. Unlike encrypting ransomware, locker ransomware does not directly encrypt files; instead, it employs tactics to restrict the victim's access to their device or specific functionalities. Some notable examples of locker ransomware include Reveton and FBI-themed ransomware.

2.2.3 Hybrid Ransomware

Hybrid ransomware combines elements of both encryption and locker ransomware. It not only encrypts the victim's files but also locks their system or specific functionalities to maximize the impact and pressure for ransom payment. By employing a combination of encryption and locking techniques, hybrid ransomware poses a significant threat to organizations and individuals.

The encryption aspect of hybrid ransomware ensures the victim's files are held hostage, while the locking feature restricts access to the system, making it more difficult for the victim to seek assistance or restore the compromised system. This combined approach increases the urgency and motivation for victims to pay the ransom. Some variants of the Cerber ransomware family have exhibited hybrid characteristics.

Understanding the different types of ransomware, including encrypting, locker, and hybrid ransomware, is crucial for organizations and individuals seeking to protect themselves from these malicious threats. Implementing a multi-layered defense strategy, including robust cybersecurity measures, regular data backups, user education and awareness, and advanced threat detection technologies, can help mitigate the risks associated with ransomware attacks. Additionally, maintaining up-to-date security software, promptly applying security patches, and regularly reviewing and enhancing security policies and procedures are essential steps in preventing and combating ransomware threats effectively.

2.3 Common Attack Vectors: Phishing, Malvertising, and Exploit Kits

Ransomware attacks employ various attack vectors to infiltrate systems and networks. Understanding these common attack vectors is essential for organizations and individuals to strengthen their defenses and mitigate the risk of falling victim to ransomware. Some of the most prevalent attack vectors include phishing, malvertising, and exploit kits.

2.3.1 Phishing

Phishing is a widely used attack vector in which attackers send fraudulent emails, messages, or other forms of communication disguised as legitimate entities. These deceptive communications often contain malicious links or attachments that, when clicked or opened, initiate the ransomware infection process. Phishing emails may appear to be from trusted sources such as banks, social media platforms, or reputable organizations, tricking users into providing sensitive information or executing malicious code.

Phishing attacks rely on social engineering techniques to exploit human vulnerability and manipulate users into taking action that compromises their systems or networks. To mitigate the risk of phishing attacks, individuals and organizations should educate themselves about phishing indicators, use email filters and spam detection software, verify the legitimacy of communication before clicking on links or opening attachments, and maintain a healthy skepticism towards unsolicited requests for sensitive information.

2.3.2 Malvertising

Malvertising, short for malicious advertising, involves the dissemination of online advertisements that contain hidden malicious code. Attackers exploit vulnerabilities in advertising networks or compromise legitimate websites to inject malicious advertisements. When users visit these compromised websites or interact with the malicious ads, the ransomware payload is delivered to their systems. Malvertising attacks often leverage drive-by downloads, where the user's device is infected automatically without any action required from the user.

To protect against malvertising attacks, individuals and organizations should consider using ad-blockers and reputable security software that detects and blocks malicious advertisements. Regularly updating browsers and plugins with the latest security patches also helps mitigate the risk of exploit-based malvertising attacks.

2.3.3 Exploit Kits

Exploit kits are malicious toolkits that exploit vulnerabilities in software or web browsers to deliver ransomware payloads. These kits are typically hosted on compromised websites and automatically scan visitors' systems for known vulnerabilities. If a vulnerable system is detected, the exploit kit deploys the appropriate exploit to deliver the ransomware payload.

Exploit kits are often distributed through malvertising campaigns, compromised websites, or malicious email attachments. To protect against exploit kit attacks, it is crucial to maintain up-to-date software and promptly apply security patches. Regular vulnerability assessments and penetration testing can also help identify and address potential vulnerabilities before they can be exploited by attackers.

Phishing, malvertising, and exploit kits are common attack vectors used by ransomware attackers to infiltrate systems and networks. Organizations and individuals should be aware of these attack vectors and implement proactive security measures to mitigate the risks associated with them. This includes user education and awareness about phishing techniques, the use of ad-blockers and security software to detect and block malicious advertisements, and maintaining up-to-date software and security patches to address vulnerabilities that exploit kits may target. By staying vigilant and implementing effective defense strategies, individuals and organizations can significantly reduce the likelihood of falling victim to ransomware attacks.

Chapter 3: Assessing Your Security Posture

In the ever-evolving landscape of ransomware threats, a proactive approach to security is essential. Before we can effectively defend against ransomware attacks, we must first assess our security posture. In this chapter, we will explore the critical process of evaluating our existing security measures, identifying vulnerabilities, and determining our readiness to defend against ransomware. By conducting a comprehensive security assessment, we lay the groundwork for implementing robust defense strategies.

Section 3.1: Conducting a Security Risk Assessment

A security risk assessment forms the foundation of a strong defense against ransomware. In this section, we will delve into the process of conducting a thorough risk assessment, evaluating the potential threats and vulnerabilities specific to our systems and environments. We will explore risk assessment frameworks, methodologies, and tools that can aid in identifying and prioritizing potential risks. By understanding our risk landscape, we can allocate resources effectively and develop targeted defense strategies.

Section 3.2: Identifying Vulnerabilities and Weak Points

No system is impervious to vulnerabilities, and identifying them is crucial to fortifying our defenses against ransomware attacks. In this section, we will explore techniques for vulnerability assessment and penetration testing, examining how these processes help identify weaknesses in our systems, networks, and applications. By systematically uncovering vulnerabilities, we can address them before attackers exploit them for their malicious purposes.

Section 3.3: Evaluating Readiness to Defend Against Ransomware

Preparing for a ransomware attack requires a thorough evaluation of our readiness to defend against such threats. In this section, we will discuss key aspects to consider when assessing our readiness. This includes evaluating the effectiveness of our backup and disaster recovery plans, reviewing the implementation of security controls such as firewalls and intrusion detection systems, and assessing employee awareness and training programs. By gauging our preparedness, we can identify areas for improvement and ensure a strong defensive posture.

Assessing our security posture is a critical step in the battle against ransomware. This chapter has explored the process of conducting a security risk assessment, identifying vulnerabilities, and evaluating our readiness to defend against ransomware attacks. Armed with the insights gained through these assessments, we can take targeted actions to strengthen our defenses, mitigate risks, and enhance our overall security posture.

As we progress through this book, we will build upon this foundation, exploring proven defense strategies and best practices to bolster our ransomware defenses. By combining a comprehensive security assessment with proactive defense measures, we can better protect our organizations and ourselves from the ever-evolving ransomware threat landscape.

Let us now embark on the journey of implementing robust defense strategies, fortified by our thorough assessment of our security posture. Together, we will build resilient defenses that can withstand the challenges posed by ransomware attacks.

3.1 Conducting a Security Risk Assessment

A security risk assessment is a systematic process that helps organizations identify, analyze, and prioritize potential security risks and vulnerabilities. By conducting a comprehensive security risk assessment, organizations can gain a clear understanding of their current security posture and develop effective strategies to mitigate risks. Here are the key steps involved in conducting a security risk assessment:

Establish the Scope and Objectives:

Clearly define the scope and objectives of the security risk assessment. Determine the assets, systems, and processes to be assessed, as well as the desired outcomes of the assessment.

Identify Assets and Data:

Identify the critical assets, information, and data within the organization. This includes physical assets (e.g., hardware, facilities), digital assets (e.g., databases, software), and sensitive information (e.g., customer data, intellectual property).

Identify Threats and Vulnerabilities:

Identify potential threats and vulnerabilities that could impact the security of the identified assets. Consider both internal and external threats, such as cyberattacks, physical breaches, insider threats, and natural disasters. Assess the vulnerabilities within the organization's infrastructure, systems, and processes that could be exploited by these threats.

Assess Impact and Likelihood:

Evaluate the potential impact of each identified threat on the organization's assets and operations. Assess the likelihood or probability of each threat occurring based on historical data, industry trends, and expert knowledge. This assessment helps prioritize risks and allocate resources effectively.

Evaluate Existing Controls:

Review the existing security controls and measures in place within the organization. Assess their effectiveness in mitigating identified risks and vulnerabilities. Identify any gaps or weaknesses in the current security measures that need to be addressed.

Analyze Risk Levels:

Analyze the identified risks based on their likelihood and potential impact. Use a risk matrix or similar method to determine the level of risk for each identified threat. Categorize risks as high, medium, or low based on their severity.

Prioritize Risks:

Prioritize the identified risks based on their risk levels and potential impact on the organization. Consider factors such as the criticality of assets, regulatory requirements, and business objectives. This helps allocate resources and prioritize mitigation efforts effectively.

Develop Mitigation Strategies:

Develop a set of strategies and controls to mitigate the identified risks. This may involve implementing technical controls, improving policies and procedures, enhancing employee training and awareness programs, or adopting new technologies. Each mitigation strategy should be tailored to address specific risks and vulnerabilities.

Implement and Monitor:

Implement the identified mitigation strategies and controls within the organization. Continuously monitor and assess the effectiveness of these measures. Regularly review and update the security risk assessment to account for new threats, changes in the organization's environment, and emerging technologies.

Document and Communicate:

Document the findings, recommendations, and action plans resulting from the security risk assessment. Communicate the assessment outcomes to relevant stakeholders, including management, IT teams, and employees. This ensures a shared understanding of the identified risks and the organization's approach to mitigating them.

Conducting a security risk assessment is a crucial step in safeguarding an organization's assets and mitigating potential risks. By following a systematic approach to identify threats, vulnerabilities, and controls, organizations can make informed decisions to strengthen their security posture. Regularly reviewing and updating the security risk assessment ensures ongoing protection against evolving threats and helps maintain a proactive and resilient security posture.

3.2 Identifying Vulnerabilities and Weak Points

Identifying vulnerabilities and weak points within an organization's systems, infrastructure, and processes is a critical step in effectively defending against ransomware attacks. By proactively identifying these weaknesses, organizations can prioritize their efforts to address and mitigate potential risks. Here are the key steps involved in identifying vulnerabilities and weak points:

Conduct Vulnerability Scanning:

Perform vulnerability scanning on the organization's networks, systems, and applications. Use automated scanning tools to identify known vulnerabilities, misconfigurations, and outdated software versions. Regular vulnerability scanning helps pinpoint areas of weakness that attackers could exploit.

Perform Penetration Testing:

Conduct penetration testing, also known as ethical hacking, to simulate real-world attacks and identify vulnerabilities that may not be detected through automated scanning. Penetration testing involves actively attempting to exploit weaknesses to gain unauthorized access or compromise systems. It provides valuable insights into potential attack vectors and vulnerabilities.

Review Security Policies and Procedures:

Evaluate the organization's security policies and procedures to identify any gaps or weaknesses. Assess if security policies align with industry best practices and regulatory requirements. Look for areas where policies may be outdated or insufficient in addressing current threats and vulnerabilities.

Assess Network Infrastructure:

Evaluate the organization's network infrastructure, including routers, switches, firewalls, and wireless networks. Look for misconfigurations, weak access controls, unauthorized network access points, or other vulnerabilities that could be exploited by attackers. Assess the effectiveness of network segmentation and access control mechanisms.

Review System Configurations:

Review system configurations, including operating systems, applications, and cloud services. Ensure that systems are configured securely and follow industry best practices. Look for default or weak passwords, unnecessary services or features, and unpatched software. Identify any system vulnerabilities that could be exploited by ransomware attacks.

Evaluate Employee Awareness and Training:

Assess the organization's employee awareness and training programs related to cybersecurity. Evaluate if employees are adequately trained on recognizing phishing attempts, social engineering techniques, and safe computing practices. Identify areas where additional training or awareness initiatives may be needed to strengthen the human factor in cybersecurity defense.

Analyze Physical Security Measures:

Assess physical security measures, such as access control systems, video surveillance, and data center security. Evaluate if these measures adequately protect sensitive areas, assets, and equipment. Look for vulnerabilities in physical security that could result in unauthorized access or compromise.

Review Incident Response Plans:

Evaluate the organization's incident response plans and procedures. Identify any weaknesses or gaps in the plans, such as unclear roles and responsibilities, outdated contact information, or insufficient processes for timely response and recovery. Ensure that the incident response plans align with industry standards and address ransomware-specific scenarios.

Stay Informed about Vulnerabilities and Threats:

Stay updated on the latest vulnerabilities, exploits, and emerging threats through reliable sources such as security advisories, industry forums, and threat intelligence feeds. Regularly monitor security news and vendor notifications to identify new vulnerabilities relevant to the organization's systems and applications.

Engage External Security Assessments:

Consider engaging external security professionals or third-party vendors to conduct independent security assessments. External assessments provide an unbiased view of an organization's security posture and can uncover vulnerabilities that may be overlooked internally.

Identifying vulnerabilities and weak points is a crucial aspect of effective ransomware defense. By conducting vulnerability scanning, performing penetration testing, reviewing security policies and procedures, evaluating network infrastructure and system configurations, assessing employee awareness and training, analyzing physical security measures, and reviewing incident response plans, organizations can identify potential weaknesses and take appropriate actions to address them. Staying informed about the latest vulnerabilities and engaging external security assessments further enhances an organization's ability to protect against ransomware attacks. Regular assessments and proactive mitigation efforts contribute to a stronger and more resilient security posture.

3.3 Evaluating Readiness to Defend Against Ransomware

Evaluating readiness to defend against ransomware is crucial to assess an organization's preparedness and identify areas that require improvement. By conducting a thorough evaluation, organizations can proactively identify gaps in their defense strategies and implement appropriate measures to enhance their resilience against ransomware attacks. Here are the key steps involved in evaluating readiness to defend against ransomware:

Assess Security Controls:

Evaluate the effectiveness of existing security controls in place within the organization. This includes examining the deployment and configuration of firewalls, intrusion detection and prevention systems, antivirus software, and endpoint security solutions. Assess if these controls are up-to-date, properly maintained, and capable of detecting and preventing ransomware attacks.

Review Backup and Recovery Processes:

Evaluate the organization's backup and recovery processes. Assess the frequency of backups, the reliability of backup systems, and the availability of offsite backups. Verify that backup files are properly protected and can be restored in a timely manner in the event of a ransomware incident. Consider conducting test restores to ensure the integrity and usability of backup data.

Evaluate Patch Management Practices:

Review the organization's patch management practices. Assess if systems and applications are regularly patched with the latest security updates and patches. Evaluate the effectiveness of the patch management process in addressing known vulnerabilities that could be exploited by ransomware attacks. Identify any gaps or delays in patch deployment and remediation.

Analyze Network Segmentation:

Assess the organization's network segmentation strategy. Evaluate if critical systems and sensitive data are appropriately segmented from the rest of the network to minimize the impact of a ransomware incident. Determine if network segmentation effectively limits lateral movement of ransomware within the network, preventing its spread to critical systems.

Evaluate Access Control Measures:

Review the organization's access control measures. Assess the strength of user authentication mechanisms, password policies, and access privileges. Verify if the principle of least privilege is enforced, granting users only the necessary access rights. Assess if multifactor authentication is implemented for sensitive accounts to prevent unauthorized access in case of credential compromise.

Assess Security Awareness and Training:

Evaluate the organization's security awareness and training programs. Assess if employees receive regular training on ransomware threats, safe computing practices, and incident reporting procedures. Evaluate the effectiveness of phishing awareness programs in educating users about the risks of social engineering attacks. Consider conducting simulated phishing campaigns to measure user awareness and responsiveness.

Review Incident Response Plans:

Evaluate the organization's incident response plans specific to ransomware incidents. Assess if the plans outline clear steps for containment, eradication, and recovery in the event of an attack. Verify if roles and responsibilities are defined, communication channels are established, and escalation procedures are in place. Assess the adequacy of technical and non-technical resources for effective incident response.

Conduct Security Awareness Assessments:

Consider conducting security awareness assessments to measure the level of security knowledge among employees. This can involve quizzes, surveys, or simulated phishing exercises.

Use the results to identify areas where additional training or awareness initiatives are needed to strengthen the human element of ransomware defense.

Evaluate Incident Reporting and Monitoring:

Assess the organization's incident reporting and monitoring capabilities. Evaluate if employees are aware of the proper channels for reporting suspicious activities or potential security incidents. Review the organization's monitoring tools and processes to detect and respond to ransomware attacks in real-time. Verify if logging and alerting mechanisms are in place to identify potential indicators of compromise.

Engage External Assessments:

Consider engaging external security experts or third-party vendors to perform independent assessments of the organization's readiness to defend against ransomware. External assessments provide an unbiased perspective and can uncover vulnerabilities or weaknesses that may be overlooked internally.

Evaluating readiness to defend against ransomware is an essential step in strengthening an organization's security posture. By assessing security controls, backup and recovery processes, patch management practices, network segmentation, access control measures, security awareness and training programs, incident response plans, incident reporting and monitoring capabilities, and engaging external assessments, organizations can identify gaps and areas for improvement. Regular evaluations and proactive measures contribute to an organization's ability to effectively defend against ransomware attacks and minimize their impact.

Chapter 4: Building a Resilient Infrastructure

In the face of ransomware attacks, a resilient infrastructure is crucial to minimizing the impact and recovering swiftly. In this chapter, we will explore the essential components and strategies for building a robust and resilient infrastructure that can withstand the challenges posed by ransomware. By implementing sound architectural principles and incorporating effective security measures, we can fortify our systems and networks against ransomware threats.

Section 4.1: Defense-in-Depth Approach

A defense-in-depth approach forms the cornerstone of a resilient infrastructure. In this section, we will delve into the concept of defense-in-depth, which involves layering multiple security measures to create overlapping lines of defense. We will discuss the importance of implementing a combination of preventive, detective, and corrective controls to minimize the risk of ransomware infiltration and mitigate its impact. By adopting a multi-layered defense strategy, we can significantly enhance the security posture of our infrastructure.

Section 4.2: Network and Endpoint Security

Ransomware attacks often target both networks and endpoints. In this section, we will explore strategies to secure our networks and endpoints effectively. We will discuss the implementation of firewalls, network segmentation, intrusion detection and prevention systems, and endpoint protection solutions. By fortifying our network and endpoints, we can create barriers that impede ransomware attackers and reduce the potential for successful attacks.

Section 4.3: Robust Backup and Disaster Recovery Strategies

A robust backup and disaster recovery plan is essential to restore operations after a ransomware attack. In this section, we will explore the key components of a comprehensive backup and recovery strategy. We will discuss backup best practices, including regular backups, off-site storage, and testing the integrity and effectiveness of backups. Additionally, we will delve into disaster recovery planning, emphasizing the importance of well-defined procedures and processes to ensure timely recovery from ransomware incidents.

Section 4.4: Secure Configurations and Access Controls

Secure configurations and access controls are critical in preventing ransomware attacks and limiting their impact. In this section, we will discuss best practices for secure configurations of systems, applications, and network devices. We will also explore the importance of implementing strong access controls, including the principle of least privilege and multi-factor authentication. By adopting secure configurations and access controls, we can reduce the attack surface and minimize the potential damage caused by ransomware.

Building a resilient infrastructure is a fundamental step in defending against ransomware attacks. This chapter has explored the importance of a defense-in-depth approach, securing networks and endpoints, implementing robust backup and disaster recovery strategies, and establishing secure configurations and access controls. By incorporating these strategies into our infrastructure, we can significantly enhance our ability to withstand ransomware attacks and recover effectively.

As we progress through this book, we will continue to explore additional defense strategies and techniques to further strengthen our ransomware defenses. By combining a resilient infrastructure with proactive defense measures, we can increase our resilience in the face of evolving ransomware threats.

Let us now embark on the journey of implementing a resilient infrastructure that can withstand ransomware attacks. Together, we will build a strong defense against this pervasive threat and protect our critical assets.

4.1 Implementing Robust Backup Strategies

Implementing robust backup strategies is essential for organizations to protect their critical data and systems from the potential impact of ransomware attacks. By having reliable and up-to-date backups, organizations can recover their data and resume operations quickly in the event of a ransomware incident. Here are the key considerations for implementing robust backup strategies:

Determine Critical Data and Systems:

Identify the critical data and systems within the organization that need to be backed up. This includes databases, file servers, application servers, and any other systems that contain important and sensitive information. Prioritize backups based on the criticality and value of the data.

Establish Backup Frequency:

Determine the frequency of backups based on the rate of data change and the acceptable data loss in case of a ransomware attack. Critical systems may require more frequent backups, while less critical systems may have lower backup frequency. Consider using incremental or differential backup methods to optimize backup efficiency.

Use Multiple Backup Locations:

Store backups in multiple locations to ensure redundancy and protection against physical and logical failures. This can include on-premises backups, offsite backups, or cloud-based backup solutions. Distributing backups across different locations minimizes the risk of losing data due to a single point of failure.

Implement Offline or Immutable Backups:

Offline backups, such as disconnected external hard drives or offline tape storage, provide protection against ransomware attacks. Since offline backups are not accessible to the network, they are immune to ransomware encryption. Immutable backup solutions, such as write-once, read-many (WORM) storage, prevent backups from being modified or deleted, adding an extra layer of protection.

Automate Backup Processes:

Implement automated backup processes to ensure consistency and reliability. Use backup software or tools that allow for scheduled backups and automation of backup jobs. Automated backups reduce the risk of human error and ensure that backups are performed regularly without manual intervention.

Verify Backup Integrity:

Regularly verify the integrity of backup data to ensure that it can be successfully restored. Perform test restores on a periodic basis to validate the backup process and confirm that the data can be recovered accurately. Monitoring and auditing backup logs can also help identify any issues or failures in the backup process.

Implement Encryption for Backup Data:

Encrypt backup data to protect it from unauthorized access or data breaches. Use strong encryption algorithms and ensure that encryption keys are securely managed. Encryption provides an additional layer of security for backup data, even if physical media or cloud storage is compromised.

Secure Backup Infrastructure:

Secure the backup infrastructure to prevent unauthorized access or tampering. Implement access controls, such as strong passwords, multi-factor authentication, and role-based access control, to protect backup systems and storage. Regularly patch and update backup software and hardware to address any known vulnerabilities.

Define Retention Policies:

Establish retention policies for backup data based on regulatory requirements, business needs, and compliance standards. Define how long backups should be retained and when they can be safely deleted. Consider legal and regulatory obligations that may require longer retention periods for certain types of data.

Test and Document the Backup and Recovery Process:

Regularly test the backup and recovery process to ensure its effectiveness. Conduct mock recovery exercises to verify the speed and accuracy of data restoration. Document the backup and recovery procedures, including step-by-step instructions, contacts, and escalation processes, to guide the recovery team during an actual ransomware incident.

Implementing robust backup strategies is a critical component of ransomware defense. By determining critical data, establishing backup frequency, using multiple backup locations, implementing offline or immutable backups, automating backup processes, verifying backup integrity, encrypting backup data, securing backup infrastructure, defining retention policies, and testing the backup and recovery process, organizations can ensure the availability and integrity of their data in the face of a ransomware attack. Proactive backup strategies significantly reduce the impact of ransomware incidents and enable organizations to recover quickly and resume normal operations.

4.2 Disaster Recovery Planning and Testing

Disaster recovery planning is a crucial aspect of ransomware defense, as it focuses on ensuring the continuity of business operations and the recovery of critical systems and data in the event of a ransomware attack. Developing a comprehensive disaster recovery plan and regularly testing its effectiveness are essential to minimize downtime and mitigate the impact of ransomware incidents. Here are the key considerations for disaster recovery planning and testing:

Business Impact Analysis:

Conduct a thorough business impact analysis (BIA) to identify critical systems, processes, and data. Determine the maximum tolerable downtime (MTD) and recovery time objectives (RTOs) for each critical component. This analysis helps prioritize recovery efforts and allocate resources effectively.

Develop a Disaster Recovery Plan:

Create a detailed disaster recovery plan that outlines the step-by-step procedures to be followed in the event of a ransomware attack. Include recovery strategies, roles and responsibilities of the recovery team, communication protocols, and a timeline for recovery activities. Ensure the plan is documented, accessible, and regularly updated.

Identify Recovery Solutions:

Determine the most appropriate recovery solutions based on the BIA and RTOs. This may include restoring systems from backups, utilizing redundant infrastructure, or leveraging cloud-based disaster recovery services. Consider the technical and operational feasibility, cost-effectiveness, and scalability of the recovery solutions.

Define Recovery Point Objectives (RPOs):

Establish recovery point objectives (RPOs) that define the acceptable amount of data loss in case of a ransomware incident. RPOs determine the frequency of backups and help align recovery strategies with business requirements. Consider the criticality of data and the potential impact of data loss on business operations.

Implement Redundancy and Resilience:

Incorporate redundancy and resilience measures to minimize the impact of ransomware attacks. This includes deploying redundant systems, implementing failover mechanisms, and diversifying infrastructure across multiple locations. Redundancy and resilience enhance the organization's ability to recover quickly and maintain essential operations.

Test the Disaster Recovery Plan:

Regularly test the effectiveness of the disaster recovery plan through simulated recovery exercises. Conduct tabletop exercises or full-scale simulations to simulate various ransomware attack scenarios and assess the response and recovery capabilities. Evaluate the plan's feasibility, identify gaps or weaknesses, and refine the plan based on the test results.

Validate Data Restoration:

During recovery testing, validate the restoration of backup data and ensure its integrity and accuracy. Test the recovery of critical systems, applications, and data to verify that they can be restored within the defined RTOs. Monitor the recovery process and document any issues or areas for improvement.

Review and Update the Plan:

Continuously review and update the disaster recovery plan to incorporate lessons learned from testing and real-world incidents. Stay informed about new ransomware threats and evolving attack techniques to adapt the plan accordingly. Regularly communicate updates to the recovery team and stakeholders.

Document Communication and Escalation Procedures:

Clearly define communication and escalation procedures within the disaster recovery plan. Establish lines of communication with key stakeholders, such as senior management, IT staff, and external service providers. Document contact information, escalation paths, and notification protocols to ensure effective and timely communication during a ransomware incident.

Provide Training and Awareness:

Train the recovery team and relevant staff on their roles and responsibilities outlined in the disaster recovery plan. Conduct awareness sessions to educate employees on the importance of disaster recovery and their individual roles in the recovery process. Regularly reinforce training to ensure preparedness and familiarity with the plan.

Disaster recovery planning and testing are essential components of ransomware defense. By conducting a business impact analysis, developing a comprehensive disaster recovery plan, identifying recovery solutions, defining RPOs, implementing redundancy and resilience, testing the plan, validating data restoration, reviewing and updating the plan, documenting communication and escalation procedures, and providing training and awareness, organizations can enhance their readiness to respond to ransomware incidents effectively. A well-prepared and tested disaster recovery plan significantly reduces downtime, minimizes data loss, and facilitates the timely restoration of critical systems and operations.

4.3 Strengthening Network Security: Firewalls, Intrusion Detection Systems (IDS), and Intrusion Prevention Systems (IPS)

Strengthening network security is essential in defending against ransomware attacks. Firewalls, Intrusion Detection Systems (IDS), and Intrusion Prevention Systems (IPS) play a crucial role in protecting networks from unauthorized access, malicious activities, and potential ransomware threats. Here are the key considerations for implementing and optimizing these security measures:

Firewalls:

Firewalls act as the first line of defense by monitoring and controlling network traffic based on predefined security rules. Consider the following best practices for firewall implementation:

a. Deploy both network-level and host-based firewalls to provide comprehensive protection.

b. Configure firewall rules to allow only necessary network traffic and block potentially malicious connections.

c. Regularly update firewall software and firmware to patch vulnerabilities and ensure the latest threat intelligence is in place.

d. Implement intrusion prevention capabilities within the firewall to detect and block known attack patterns.

e. Enable logging and monitoring features to track and analyze network traffic for potential security incidents.

Intrusion Detection Systems (IDS):

IDS monitors network traffic, detects suspicious activities, and generates alerts for potential security breaches. Consider the following practices for IDS implementation:

a. Deploy both network-based and host-based IDS to detect attacks at different levels of the network.

b. Configure IDS to monitor critical network segments, such as DMZs and internal networks, where sensitive systems and data reside.

c. Regularly update IDS signatures and rulesets to detect new and evolving ransomware threats.

d. Establish appropriate alerting and notification mechanisms to ensure timely response to detected threats.

e. Integrate IDS with other security tools and systems for enhanced threat visibility and correlation of security events.

Intrusion Prevention Systems (IPS):

IPS goes beyond IDS by actively blocking and preventing malicious activities in real-time. Consider the following practices for IPS implementation:

a. Deploy network-based and host-based IPS to provide comprehensive protection across the network infrastructure.

b. Configure IPS to actively block suspicious traffic and known attack signatures, including ransomware-related behaviors.

c. Regularly update IPS signatures and rulesets to stay current with emerging threats.

d. Implement inline IPS deployments for immediate threat mitigation and prevention.

e. Continuously monitor and fine-tune IPS settings to minimize false positives and false negatives.

Network Segmentation:

Implement network segmentation to isolate critical systems and sensitive data from other parts of the network. Consider the following practices for effective network segmentation:

a. Divide the network into separate segments based on security requirements and data sensitivity.

b. Use firewalls and access control lists (ACLs) to control and restrict traffic between network segments.

c. Apply the principle of least privilege by granting network access only to authorized users and systems.

d. Implement network segmentation along with VLANs, subnets, or virtualization technologies to create logical boundaries.

Regular Vulnerability Assessments:

Conduct regular vulnerability assessments to identify and address potential weaknesses in the network infrastructure. Consider the following practices for vulnerability assessments:

a. Use automated scanning tools to identify vulnerabilities and misconfigurations in network devices, systems, and applications.

b. Prioritize vulnerability remediation based on risk severity and potential impact on ransomware defense.

c. Implement a robust patch management process to address identified vulnerabilities promptly.

d. Perform periodic penetration testing to assess the effectiveness of network security controls.

Network Monitoring and Incident Response:

Implement robust network monitoring and incident response capabilities to detect and respond to ransomware threats. Consider the following practices:

a. Implement network traffic monitoring tools to identify anomalous behavior and potential indicators of ransomware attacks.

b. Establish an incident response plan with clear roles, responsibilities, and escalation procedures.

c. Conduct regular security awareness training to educate employees about the risks of ransomware and the importance of reporting suspicious activities.

d. Implement network-based behavioral analysis tools to detect deviations from normal network behavior.

By implementing firewalls, IDS, IPS, network segmentation, regular vulnerability assessments, network monitoring, and incident response capabilities, organizations can strengthen their network security and enhance their defenses against ransomware attacks. These security measures collectively contribute to early threat detection, rapid response, and effective mitigation of ransomware incidents, safeguarding critical systems and data from unauthorized access and malicious activities.

4.4 Enhancing Endpoint Security: Antivirus, Endpoint Detection and Response (EDR), and Host-based Firewalls

Enhancing endpoint security is crucial in protecting individual devices and endpoints from ransomware attacks. Antivirus software, Endpoint Detection and Response (EDR) solutions, and host-based firewalls play a vital role in safeguarding endpoints from malicious activities and minimizing the risk of ransomware infections. Here are the key considerations for implementing and optimizing these endpoint security measures:

Antivirus Software:

Antivirus software is a fundamental component of endpoint security that helps detect and remove known malware, including ransomware. Consider the following practices for antivirus implementation:

a. Deploy reputable antivirus software across all endpoints and ensure it is regularly updated with the latest virus definitions.

b. Enable real-time scanning to detect and block malicious files and activities as they occur.

c. Configure scheduled system scans to proactively identify and eliminate malware threats.

d. Implement behavior-based detection to identify suspicious activities and potential ransomware behaviors.

e. Integrate antivirus software with centralized management consoles for easy monitoring and administration.

Endpoint Detection and Response (EDR):

EDR solutions provide advanced threat detection and response capabilities, enabling organizations to detect and respond to ransomware attacks in real-time. Consider the following practices for EDR implementation:

a. Deploy EDR solutions on endpoints to monitor and analyze system activities, network traffic, and user behavior for potential ransomware threats.

b. Leverage machine learning and behavioral analysis techniques to identify anomalies and indicators of compromise (IOCs).

c. Enable threat hunting capabilities to proactively search for ransomware-related IOCs and indicators of attack (IOAs).

d. Implement automated response actions, such as quarantining or isolating compromised endpoints, to prevent the spread of ransomware.

e. Regularly review EDR logs and alerts to identify potential security incidents and respond swiftly.

Host-based Firewalls:

Host-based firewalls provide an additional layer of defense by controlling inbound and outbound network traffic at the endpoint level. Consider the following practices for host-based firewall implementation:

a. Enable host-based firewalls on all endpoints to filter network traffic and block unauthorized connections.

b. Configure firewall rules to allow only necessary network communications and block suspicious or malicious activities.

c. Regularly update firewall rules to address emerging threats and vulnerabilities.

d. Implement application-level filtering to control access to specific applications and services.

e. Monitor host-based firewall logs for suspicious network activities and potential indicators of ransomware attacks.

Patch Management:

Keeping endpoints up to date with the latest patches and security updates is crucial in preventing ransomware attacks. Consider the following practices for effective patch management:

a. Establish a patch management process to regularly identify and deploy software updates, security patches, and firmware updates for endpoints.

b. Prioritize critical security patches and updates related to the operating system, antivirus software, web browsers, and other commonly targeted applications.

c. Test patches in a controlled environment before deployment to ensure compatibility and minimize the risk of system disruptions.

d. Automate patch deployment whenever possible to streamline the process and reduce manual errors.

e. Implement vulnerability scanning tools to identify endpoints that require patching and monitor compliance with patching policies.

User Privilege Management:

Restricting user privileges and implementing the principle of least privilege is essential in minimizing the impact of ransomware attacks. Consider the following practices for user privilege management:

a. Implement strong access controls and user authentication mechanisms to prevent unauthorized access to critical endpoints.

b. Assign users the minimum level of privileges required to perform their tasks effectively.

c. Implement administrative access controls to restrict the execution of potentially malicious files and scripts.

d. Regularly review user privileges and remove unnecessary administrative rights.

e. Implement user behavior monitoring to detect suspicious activities and potential misuse of privileges.

By implementing antivirus software, EDR solutions, host-based firewalls, effective patch management, and user privilege management, organizations can significantly enhance endpoint security and reduce the risk of ransomware infections. These endpoint security measures work together to detect and respond to ransomware threats, mitigate the impact of attacks, and protect critical data and systems from compromise.

4.5 Secure Configurations and Access Controls: Patch Management, Least Privilege, and Network Segmentation

Implementing secure configurations and access controls is crucial for strengthening defenses against ransomware attacks. Proper patch management, implementing the principle of least privilege, and network segmentation help minimize vulnerabilities, limit the impact of potential breaches, and prevent the spread of ransomware. Here are the key considerations for implementing secure configurations and access controls:

Patch Management:

Patch management involves regularly updating software, operating systems, and firmware to address known vulnerabilities. Consider the following practices for effective patch management:

a. Establish a patch management process that includes identifying, testing, and deploying patches across all systems and endpoints.

b. Prioritize critical security patches that address known vulnerabilities frequently targeted by ransomware attacks.

c. Automate patch deployment whenever possible to ensure timely updates and minimize human error.

d. Test patches in a controlled environment before deploying them to production systems to mitigate potential disruptions.

e. Monitor and track patch compliance to identify any missed or failed patches.

Principle of Least Privilege:

The principle of least privilege restricts user access rights to the bare minimum necessary for their tasks. Consider the following practices for implementing the principle of least privilege:

a. Regularly review user access rights and permissions, removing unnecessary privileges.

b. Implement strong authentication mechanisms, such as multi-factor authentication, to prevent unauthorized access.

c. Assign users to appropriate access groups based on their job roles and responsibilities.

d. Monitor user activity and enforce policies to prevent users from escalating privileges without proper authorization.

e. Educate users about the importance of the principle of least privilege and the risks associated with excessive access rights.

Network Segmentation:

Network segmentation involves dividing the network into isolated segments to limit the lateral movement of ransomware and contain potential breaches. Consider the following practices for network segmentation:

a. Identify critical assets, sensitive data, and high-risk systems that require additional protection.

b. Implement separate network segments for different departments, functions, or security zones.

c. Use firewalls and access control lists (ACLs) to control traffic between network segments.

d. Monitor network traffic and implement intrusion detection and prevention systems (IDS/IPS) at segment boundaries.

e. Implement network segmentation best practices, such as using VLANs, subnets, or virtualization technologies.

Secure Configuration Management:

Implementing secure configurations helps reduce vulnerabilities and strengthen overall security posture. Consider the following practices for secure configuration management:

a. Follow security best practices and vendor guidelines when configuring systems, applications, and network devices.

b. Disable or remove unnecessary services, protocols, and features that may introduce security risks.

c. Regularly review and update system configurations to align with evolving security requirements.

d. Implement centralized configuration management tools to ensure consistent and secure configurations across all endpoints.

e. Regularly audit and monitor system configurations to detect and remediate any deviations from secure standards.

Access Controls and Privileged Account Management:

Implement strong access controls and proper privileged account management to prevent unauthorized access and limit the impact of ransomware attacks. Consider the following practices:

a. Implement strong password policies and enforce regular password changes.

b. Utilize privileged access management (PAM) solutions to securely manage and monitor privileged accounts.

c. Implement session monitoring and recording for privileged accounts to track activities and detect suspicious behavior.

d. Implement two-factor authentication for privileged accounts to add an extra layer of security.

e. Regularly review and audit access controls and privileges to ensure compliance with security policies.

By implementing secure configurations, patch management practices, the principle of least privilege, network segmentation, and robust access controls, organizations can significantly enhance their defenses against ransomware attacks. These measures minimize vulnerabilities, limit the impact of potential breaches, and prevent the lateral movement of ransomware across the network. By adopting a proactive approach to security configuration and access controls, organizations can reduce the risk of ransomware infections and protect their critical systems and data from compromise.

Chapter 5: User Awareness and Training

In the battle against ransomware, users play a crucial role as the first line of defense. Educating and empowering users to recognize and mitigate ransomware risks is essential to creating a resilient security culture. In this chapter, we will explore the importance of user awareness and training in the context of ransomware defense. We will discuss strategies for raising awareness, providing effective training, and promoting secure practices among users. By equipping users with the knowledge and skills to detect and respond to ransomware threats, we strengthen our collective defense against this ever-present danger.

Section 5.1: Understanding Ransomware Risks

To combat ransomware effectively, users must understand the risks they face. In this section, we will delve into the nature of ransomware, its impact, and the potential consequences of falling victim to an attack. By explaining the anatomy of ransomware attacks and the importance of user vigilance, we lay the groundwork for cultivating a security-conscious mindset among users.

Section 5.2: Developing an Effective User Training Program

A comprehensive user training program is essential for fostering a security-aware culture. In this section, we will discuss strategies for developing and delivering effective training sessions. We will explore topics such as identifying phishing attempts, recognizing suspicious email attachments, practicing safe web browsing habits, and understanding social engineering techniques. By providing users with practical knowledge and hands-on training, we empower them to make informed decisions and become active participants in ransomware defense.

Section 5.3: Promoting Secure Practices and Behavior

Changing user behavior is crucial in mitigating the risk of ransomware attacks. In this section, we will explore strategies for promoting secure practices among users. We will discuss the importance of regularly updating software and operating systems, using strong and unique passwords, implementing two-factor authentication, and being cautious when downloading and installing applications. By emphasizing the significance of these secure practices, we can create a culture of vigilance that minimizes the opportunities for ransomware attacks.

Section 5.4: Incident Reporting and Response

Prompt and accurate reporting of potential ransomware incidents is vital for effective response and containment. In this section, we will discuss the importance of establishing clear incident reporting procedures and communication channels. We will explore how users can identify and report potential ransomware indicators, ensuring swift action can be taken to contain and mitigate the impact of an attack.

User awareness and training are indispensable in the fight against ransomware. This chapter has highlighted the importance of understanding ransomware risks, developing an effective user training program, promoting secure practices and behavior, and establishing incident reporting procedures. By investing in user awareness and training, we empower individuals to become active defenders and create a resilient human firewall against ransomware attacks.

As we continue our journey through this book, we will explore additional defense strategies and techniques to strengthen our ransomware defenses. By combining user awareness and training with technical safeguards, we build a robust defense posture that can better withstand the evolving ransomware threat landscape.

Let us now embark on the path of educating and empowering users to be vigilant and proactive in the face of ransomware. Together, we will build a formidable defense against this pervasive threat and safeguard our digital assets.

5.1 Ransomware Education and Awareness Programs

Ransomware education and awareness programs are essential in equipping individuals within organizations with the knowledge and skills to identify and respond to ransomware threats. These programs aim to educate employees about the risks associated with ransomware, raise awareness about common attack vectors, and promote best practices for prevention and response. Here are the key components of an effective ransomware education and awareness program:

Ransomware Basics:

Start by providing a comprehensive overview of what ransomware is, how it works, and the potential impact it can have on individuals and organizations. Explain the different types of ransomware, encryption techniques used, and common methods of infection. Ensure that participants understand the motivations of ransomware attackers and the potential consequences of falling victim to an attack.

Phishing Awareness:

Emphasize the role of phishing attacks as one of the primary entry points for ransomware infections. Teach participants how to identify phishing emails, recognize suspicious attachments or links, and verify the legitimacy of email senders. Train employees on the importance of never clicking on suspicious links or downloading attachments from unknown sources.

Safe Internet Practices:

Educate employees about safe internet practices to minimize the risk of ransomware infections. Teach them to avoid visiting malicious websites, downloading unauthorized software or files, and clicking on pop-up advertisements. Emphasize the importance of keeping software and web browsers up to date and enabling automatic updates to patch security vulnerabilities.

Social Engineering Awareness:

Raise awareness about social engineering tactics used by attackers to manipulate individuals into unknowingly installing ransomware. Train employees to recognize common social engineering techniques, such as impersonation, pretexting, and baiting. Teach them to be cautious of unsolicited requests for sensitive information and to verify the legitimacy of requests before providing any personal or confidential data.

Best Practices for Email and File Attachments:

Provide guidelines for handling email attachments and files to minimize the risk of ransomware infections. Teach employees not to open attachments from unknown sources or those that seem suspicious, even if they appear to come from familiar contacts. Encourage the use of file scanning tools to check for malware before opening any attachments.

Secure Password Practices:

Educate employees about the importance of strong and unique passwords. Teach them to create complex passwords that include a combination of letters, numbers, and special characters. Encourage the use of password managers to securely store and generate strong passwords. Emphasize the significance of never sharing passwords and regularly updating them.

Incident Reporting Procedures:

Train employees on the proper procedures for reporting potential ransomware incidents or suspicious activities. Establish clear channels for reporting, such as a dedicated email address or a designated IT helpdesk. Encourage employees to report any phishing attempts, suspicious emails, or unusual system behaviors promptly to the appropriate personnel.

Regular Training and Updates:

Ransomware threats evolve rapidly, so it is crucial to provide regular training sessions and updates to keep employees informed about the latest attack techniques and prevention strategies. Conduct periodic refresher training sessions and stay up to date with emerging trends and best practices in ransomware defense.

Mock Phishing Exercises:

Conduct mock phishing exercises to assess the effectiveness of the education and awareness program. Simulate phishing attacks to test employees' ability to identify and report suspicious emails accurately. Provide feedback and additional training based on the results of these exercises to further strengthen their awareness and response capabilities.

Continuous Communication and Engagement:

Foster a culture of cybersecurity awareness by maintaining ongoing communication about ransomware threats and prevention measures. Use various channels, such as email newsletters, posters, intranet portals, and internal messaging systems, to regularly share updates, tips, and reminders about ransomware defense. Encourage employees to ask questions, provide feedback, and share their experiences to promote continuous learning and improvement.

A well-designed ransomware education and awareness program can significantly reduce the risk of successful ransomware attacks by equipping employees with the knowledge and skills to detect and respond to threats. By promoting a security-conscious culture, organizations can create a strong line of defense against ransomware, ensuring the protection of critical data and systems.

5.2 Best Practices for Email Security

Email is one of the most common vectors for ransomware attacks, making email security a critical component of any ransomware defense strategy. By following best practices for email security, individuals and organizations can significantly reduce the risk of falling victim to ransomware. Here are key practices to consider:

Use Strong Email Authentication:

Implement email authentication protocols like SPF (Sender Policy Framework), DKIM (DomainKeys Identified Mail), and DMARC (Domain-based Message Authentication, Reporting, and

Conformance) to verify the authenticity of incoming emails. These protocols help prevent email spoofing and ensure that emails are sent from legitimate sources.

Enable Anti-Spam and Anti-Malware Filters:

Configure robust spam filters and anti-malware scanners on email servers or email security gateways. These filters can detect and block malicious emails, attachments, and links, reducing the chances of ransomware infections through email.

Be Cautious of Phishing Attempts:

Be vigilant and skeptical of emails requesting personal information, login credentials, or financial details. Look for red flags such as misspellings, grammatical errors, or suspicious email addresses. Avoid clicking on links or downloading attachments from unfamiliar or suspicious sources. When in doubt, contact the sender directly to verify the legitimacy of the email.

Educate Users on Phishing Awareness:

Provide regular training and awareness programs to educate users about the risks associated with phishing attacks. Teach employees how to identify common phishing indicators, such as urgent or threatening language, requests for sensitive information, or unexpected attachments or links. Encourage employees to report any suspicious emails promptly.

Implement Email Encryption:

Use email encryption technologies, such as Transport Layer Security (TLS) or Secure/Multipurpose Internet Mail Extensions (S/MIME), to protect sensitive information and ensure secure email communication. Encryption helps prevent unauthorized access and ensures that email content cannot be intercepted or tampered with in transit.

Regularly Update Email Clients and Software:

Keep email clients and software up to date with the latest security patches and updates. Regular updates help address vulnerabilities and protect against known exploits that ransomware attackers may exploit.

Use Strong and Unique Passwords:

Use strong and unique passwords for email accounts to prevent unauthorized access. Avoid using common or easily guessable passwords. Consider using password managers to securely store and generate complex passwords for better account security.

Enable Two-Factor Authentication (2FA):

Implement two-factor authentication for email accounts to provide an additional layer of security. 2FA requires users to provide a second verification factor, such as a temporary code sent to a mobile device, in addition to the password.

Regularly Backup Email Data:

Regularly back up email data to ensure that critical information is not lost in the event of a ransomware attack or other data loss incidents. Backups should be stored securely and tested periodically to ensure they can be restored successfully.

Establish Email Usage Policies:

Develop and enforce email usage policies that define acceptable practices and behavior. These policies can include guidelines for handling suspicious emails, reporting procedures for potential threats, and rules for sharing sensitive information via email.

Implementing best practices for email security is crucial in mitigating the risk of ransomware attacks. By following these guidelines, individuals and organizations can create a more secure email environment, minimize the likelihood of falling victim to phishing attempts, and protect critical data and systems from ransomware infections.

5.3 Safe Web Browsing and Downloading Practices

Safe web browsing and downloading practices are essential for minimizing the risk of ransomware infections. By following best practices when accessing and downloading content from the internet, individuals and organizations can significantly reduce their exposure to malicious websites and files. Here are key practices to consider:

Keep Web Browsers and Plugins Up to Date:

Regularly update web browsers and plugins (such as Adobe Flash, Java, and Silverlight) with the latest security patches. Outdated software can contain vulnerabilities that ransomware attackers may exploit.

Enable Pop-Up Blockers:

Enable pop-up blockers in web browsers to prevent potentially malicious pop-ups from appearing. These pop-ups may contain malicious links or attempt to trick users into downloading ransomware.

Verify Website Security:

Before entering sensitive information or downloading files from a website, verify its security. Look for a padlock icon in the browser's address bar and ensure that the website URL starts with "https://" instead of "http://". The "s" in "https" indicates that the connection is encrypted and secure.

Exercise Caution with Email Links and Attachments:

Be cautious when clicking on links or downloading attachments from emails, especially from unknown or suspicious senders. Verify the legitimacy of the email and its attachments before taking any action. When in doubt, contact the sender directly to confirm the authenticity.

Beware of Phishing Websites:

Be vigilant for phishing websites that attempt to mimic legitimate websites to steal personal information. Check the URL carefully for any misspellings or variations that may indicate a fraudulent site. Avoid entering personal or sensitive information on unfamiliar websites.

Use Reputable Download Sources:

Download files and software only from reputable sources such as official websites, app stores, or trusted download platforms. Avoid downloading files from unfamiliar or suspicious websites, as they may contain malware or ransomware.

Scan Downloads for Malware:

Before opening or executing downloaded files, scan them with reliable antivirus software or malware scanners. This helps detect any potential threats and prevents ransomware infections.

Be Cautious of File-Sharing Networks:

Exercise caution when using peer-to-peer (P2P) file-sharing networks, as they can be a breeding ground for malware-infected files. Verify the authenticity and integrity of files before downloading or opening them.

Enable Browser Security Features:

Take advantage of built-in browser security features, such as safe browsing or reputation-based filtering. These features can help identify and block known malicious websites or downloads.

Regularly Update Security Software:

Keep your antivirus and anti-malware software up to date with the latest virus definitions and security patches. Regularly perform system scans to detect and remove any potential threats.

Adopting safe web browsing and downloading practices is crucial for protecting against ransomware infections. By following these best practices, individuals and organizations can minimize the risk of encountering malicious websites or downloading infected files. Staying vigilant, keeping software up to date, and using reliable security tools are key steps in maintaining a secure online browsing and downloading experience.

5.4 Secure File Sharing and Collaboration

Secure file sharing and collaboration are essential for protecting sensitive data and preventing unauthorized access or exposure to ransomware threats. By implementing secure practices and utilizing appropriate tools, individuals and organizations can maintain the confidentiality and integrity of shared files. Here are key practices for secure file sharing and collaboration:

Use Trusted File Sharing Platforms:

Choose reputable and secure file sharing platforms that employ robust encryption and security measures. Ensure that the platform encrypts data both at rest and in transit, and that it offers access controls and permissions to limit who can view, edit, or download shared files.

Encrypt Files Before Sharing:

Encrypt sensitive files before sharing them, especially when sharing them outside of trusted networks or platforms. Use strong encryption algorithms and consider using password-protected archives or file encryption tools to add an extra layer of security.

Implement Access Controls:

Set granular access controls and permissions for shared files to restrict access to authorized individuals. Only grant access to those who need it and regularly review and update access privileges to align with changing roles or responsibilities.

Use Secure File Transfer Protocols:

Utilize secure file transfer protocols such as SFTP (Secure File Transfer Protocol) or FTPS (FTP Secure) for transferring files over the internet. These protocols encrypt data during transit and provide a secure channel for transferring sensitive files.

Educate Users on Sharing Best Practices:

Educate users about best practices for sharing files securely. Train them on the importance of not sharing files through insecure channels like unencrypted email attachments or public file sharing services.

Encourage the use of designated secure platforms for file sharing and collaboration.

Implement Version Control:

Use version control mechanisms to track changes made to shared files and maintain a history of revisions. This helps prevent accidental overwrites or unauthorized modifications and allows for easy recovery in case of file corruption or ransomware attacks.

Regularly Backup Shared Files:

Ensure that shared files are regularly backed up to a secure and separate location. Implement a robust backup strategy that includes both local and offsite backups. Regularly test and verify the integrity of backups to ensure their recoverability in the event of a ransomware incident.

Train Users on Phishing Awareness:

Ransomware attacks often start with phishing emails targeting users. Educate users about phishing awareness and train them to recognize and report suspicious emails that may lead to ransomware infections. Provide guidance on identifying phishing indicators and avoiding potential traps.

Monitor and Detect Anomalies:

Implement monitoring mechanisms to detect suspicious activities or anomalies related to file sharing and collaboration. Use security tools that can identify unusual file access patterns, unauthorized sharing attempts, or unexpected changes to file permissions.

Enforce Strong Passwords and Multi-Factor Authentication (MFA):

Require strong passwords for accessing shared files and encourage the use of multi-factor authentication (MFA) for added security. MFA provides an additional layer of protection by requiring users to provide a second form of authentication, such as a temporary code or biometric verification, along with their passwords.

Secure file sharing and collaboration practices are vital for protecting sensitive data from ransomware threats. By following these best practices, individuals and organizations can ensure that shared files remain confidential, integrity is maintained, and unauthorized access is prevented. By combining user education, secure platforms, access controls, and monitoring mechanisms, file sharing and collaboration can be conducted in a safe and secure manner.

Chapter 6: Incident Response and Recovery

Despite our best efforts, ransomware incidents may still occur. In such situations, a well-defined incident response and recovery plan becomes crucial. In this chapter, we will explore the key elements of an effective incident response strategy to swiftly detect, contain, and mitigate the impact of a ransomware attack. We will also delve into the recovery phase, focusing on restoring systems and data while minimizing downtime. By preparing for the worst-case scenario and implementing a robust incident response and recovery plan, we can minimize the damage caused by ransomware and expedite the return to normal operations.

Section 6.1: Incident Response Framework

An incident response framework provides a structured approach to handling ransomware incidents. In this section, we will discuss the key components of an incident response plan, including roles and responsibilities, communication protocols, and escalation procedures. We will also explore the importance of establishing incident response teams and conducting regular drills and exercises to ensure readiness. By following a well-defined framework, organizations can effectively respond to ransomware incidents and mitigate their impact.

Section 6.2: Incident Detection and Analysis

Early detection and analysis of ransomware incidents are critical to minimizing the damage. In this section, we will explore strategies for detecting ransomware infections, including monitoring for suspicious network traffic, analyzing system logs, and leveraging threat intelligence. We will also discuss incident analysis techniques to understand the scope and impact of the attack. By swiftly detecting and analyzing ransomware incidents, organizations can initiate timely response actions and mitigate the spread of the attack.

Section 6.3: Incident Containment and Eradication

Containing a ransomware incident is essential to prevent further damage and stop the attacker's progress. In this section, we will discuss strategies for isolating infected systems, disconnecting compromised devices from the network, and disabling compromised user accounts. We will also explore techniques for eradicating the ransomware from affected systems and ensuring the removal of any persistence mechanisms. By effectively containing and eradicating the ransomware, organizations can minimize its impact and reduce the chances of reinfection.

Section 6.4: Recovery and Restoration

Once the ransomware incident is contained and eradicated, the focus shifts to recovery and restoration. In this section, we will explore strategies for recovering encrypted data from backups, validating the integrity of restored data, and restoring systems to a fully operational state. We will also discuss the importance of conducting thorough post-incident analysis to identify lessons learned and make necessary improvements to prevent future incidents. By implementing a well-planned recovery and restoration process, organizations can expedite the return to normal operations.

Incident response and recovery are critical components of an effective ransomware defense strategy. This chapter has explored the key elements of incident response, including incident detection and analysis, containment and eradication, and recovery and restoration. By preparing and implementing a robust incident response and recovery plan, organizations can minimize the impact of ransomware incidents and restore normal operations promptly.

As we progress through this book, we will continue to explore additional defense strategies and techniques to strengthen our ransomware defenses. By combining incident response and recovery with proactive preventive measures, we build a comprehensive defense posture that enhances our resilience to ransomware attacks.

Let us now prepare ourselves with a well-defined incident response and recovery plan, equipped to handle ransomware incidents with confidence. Together, we will overcome the challenges posed by ransomware and ensure the continuity and security of our digital assets.

6.1 Developing an Incident Response Plan

Developing a comprehensive incident response plan is crucial for effectively responding to ransomware attacks and minimizing their impact on organizations. An incident response plan provides a structured and coordinated approach to detecting, containing, eradicating, and recovering from ransomware incidents. Here are key steps in developing an incident response plan:

Establish an Incident Response Team:

Identify and assemble a dedicated incident response team comprising individuals from relevant departments, including IT, security, legal, and communication. Assign roles and responsibilities to team members to ensure clear lines of communication and efficient incident handling.

Define Incident Response Goals and Objectives:

Clearly define the goals and objectives of the incident response plan. These may include minimizing downtime, preserving data integrity, ensuring business continuity, mitigating reputational damage, and complying with legal and regulatory requirements.

Identify and Document Potential Ransomware Incidents:

Identify different types of ransomware incidents that may occur and document their potential impact on the organization. This includes understanding the various ransomware variants, their attack vectors, and the potential consequences for critical systems and data.

Establish Incident Classification and Severity Levels:

Develop a classification system for categorizing incidents based on their severity and potential impact. This classification helps prioritize incident response activities and allocate resources effectively.

Develop Incident Response Procedures:

Define step-by-step procedures for responding to ransomware incidents. This includes incident detection, notification, containment, eradication, recovery, and post-incident analysis. Ensure that the procedures are well-documented, easily accessible, and regularly updated.

Implement Incident Detection and Monitoring:

Deploy advanced threat detection tools and monitoring systems to detect ransomware incidents in real-time. Implement robust network and endpoint monitoring, intrusion detection systems (IDS), and security information and event management (SIEM) solutions to identify potential threats promptly.

Establish Communication and Reporting Protocols:

Define communication channels and reporting protocols to ensure effective and timely communication during a ransomware incident. Determine who needs to be notified, both internally and externally, and establish communication channels with stakeholders, including executive management, IT teams, legal advisors, and law enforcement, if necessary.

Coordinate with External Partners and Service Providers:

Establish relationships with external partners, such as incident response teams, cybersecurity firms, and law enforcement agencies. Define the process for engaging external support in case of a severe ransomware incident that requires specialized expertise or legal assistance.

Conduct Regular Incident Response Drills and Training:

Regularly conduct incident response drills and simulations to test the effectiveness of the plan and identify areas for improvement. Provide comprehensive training to incident response team members and relevant employees to ensure they are well-prepared to handle ransomware incidents.

Continuously Evaluate and Update the Plan:

Incident response plans should be treated as living documents that are regularly evaluated and updated to reflect evolving ransomware threats and organizational changes. Conduct periodic reviews and assessments to identify gaps, lessons learned, and emerging best practices to enhance the plan's effectiveness.

Developing an incident response plan is essential for effectively mitigating the impact of ransomware attacks. By establishing a well-defined plan, organizations can respond promptly and effectively, minimizing the damage and disruption caused by ransomware incidents. Regularly reviewing and updating the plan, conducting drills, and ensuring coordination with external partners are crucial for maintaining the plan's effectiveness in an ever-changing threat landscape.

6.2 Initial Response and Containment Strategies

The initial response and containment phase of an incident response plan is critical for minimizing the impact of a ransomware attack and preventing its spread throughout the organization. This phase focuses on swift action to isolate and contain the infected systems, mitigate further damage, and initiate the recovery process. Here are key strategies for the initial response and containment phase:

Activate the Incident Response Team:

Immediately activate the incident response team upon detection of a ransomware incident. Ensure that team members are aware of their roles and responsibilities and that communication channels are open and accessible.

Isolate Infected Systems:

Isolate the infected systems from the network to prevent the ransomware from spreading further. Disconnect affected devices from the network, disable their network interfaces, or isolate them in a separate network segment.

Preserve System and Network Information:

Preserve and document system and network information relevant to the incident, including timestamps, logs, and any available evidence. This information can assist in understanding the attack, identifying the ransomware variant, and determining the initial infection vector.

Determine the Scope of the Incident:

Conduct a thorough investigation to determine the extent of the ransomware infection. Identify all affected systems, files, and network shares. Assess the potential impact on critical infrastructure, data, and operations.

Notify Relevant Stakeholders:

Notify key stakeholders, including executive management, IT teams, legal counsel, and relevant personnel, about the incident. Provide them with initial information about the situation, potential impact, and ongoing response efforts.

Implement Backup Restoration:

Begin restoring affected systems and files from secure and verified backups. Ensure that backups are not compromised or infected with ransomware. Verify the integrity and completeness of backups before initiating the restoration process.

Assess the Need for External Assistance:

Evaluate the need for external assistance, such as engaging incident response service providers or contacting law enforcement agencies. Consider involving cybersecurity experts who specialize in ransomware incidents for guidance and support.

Implement Temporary Workarounds:

If critical systems are affected, implement temporary workarounds or alternate procedures to maintain essential business operations. This may involve deploying temporary infrastructure, accessing data from unaffected backups, or employing manual processes.

Implement Access Controls and Password Resets:

Change all passwords associated with compromised accounts and systems. Implement strong access controls, including two-factor authentication, to prevent unauthorized access during the recovery process.

Communicate Internally and Externally:

Maintain open lines of communication with employees, stakeholders, and external parties such as customers, partners, and regulatory authorities. Provide regular updates on the incident, response efforts, and mitigation measures.

Document the Initial Response:

Document all actions taken during the initial response and containment phase. This documentation will serve as a valuable reference for post-incident analysis, compliance reporting, and potential legal investigations.

Collect Forensic Evidence:

Preserve and collect forensic evidence, including system logs, network traffic captures, and malware samples. This evidence can aid in identifying the attackers, their tactics, and potential vulnerabilities that were exploited.

The initial response and containment phase is a critical part of the incident response plan, aiming to swiftly isolate and contain a ransomware attack. By activating the incident response team, isolating infected systems, preserving system information, and implementing backup restoration, organizations can effectively limit the impact and initiate the recovery process. Clear communication, temporary workarounds, and the documentation of actions taken are essential for maintaining transparency and ensuring a coordinated response effort.

6.3 Mitigation and Removal of Ransomware

Once the initial response and containment phase is completed, the focus shifts to mitigating the impact of the ransomware attack and removing the malware from the affected systems. This phase involves a combination of technical measures, thorough investigation, and remediation efforts. Here are key strategies for mitigating and removing ransomware:

Identify and Quarantine Infected Systems:

Identify all systems infected with ransomware and quarantine them from the network to prevent further damage and data loss. Disconnect infected devices from the network or isolate them in a separate network segment.

Disable or Remove the Ransomware:

Disable or remove the ransomware from infected systems. Use reputable antivirus or antimalware software to scan and remove the malware. Ensure that the software is up to date with the latest virus definitions.

Recover Systems from Clean Backups:

Restore affected systems and files from clean and verified backups. Prioritize critical systems and data, ensuring that backups are free from malware. Validate the integrity of backups before performing the restoration process.

Patch Vulnerabilities and Update Software:

Identify and patch vulnerabilities that were exploited by the ransomware to gain access. Keep all software and operating systems up to date with the latest security patches and updates to mitigate potential entry points for future attacks.

Implement Network Segmentation:

Enhance network segmentation to isolate critical systems and sensitive data from potential ransomware infections. Divide the network into segments with separate access controls and restrict lateral movement within the network.

Strengthen Security Controls:

Review and strengthen existing security controls, such as firewalls, intrusion detection systems (IDS), and intrusion prevention systems (IPS). Ensure that these controls are properly configured, regularly updated, and actively monitoring network traffic.

Conduct Thorough System Scans:

Perform thorough system scans to identify any remnants or hidden traces of the ransomware. Use reputable scanning tools to detect and remove any remaining malware components or malicious artifacts.

Analyze and Investigate the Incident:

Conduct a detailed analysis and investigation of the ransomware incident. Identify the initial infection vector, determine the extent of the attack, and assess the impact on systems, data, and operations. Collect and analyze logs, network traffic, and any available forensic evidence.

Apply Security Enhancements:

Implement security enhancements based on the findings of the investigation. This may include strengthening access controls, tightening security configurations, implementing additional security measures, and enhancing user awareness and training programs.

Update Incident Response Plan:

Incorporate lessons learned from the ransomware incident into the incident response plan. Revise and update the plan to address any identified gaps, improve response procedures, and enhance the organization's ability to mitigate and respond to future ransomware incidents.

Educate Employees:

Provide comprehensive training and awareness programs to educate employees about ransomware threats, safe computing practices, and how to identify and report potential security incidents. Regularly reinforce the importance of security measures and the role that employees play in maintaining a secure environment.

Continuously Monitor and Test Systems:

Implement continuous monitoring and regular testing of systems and networks to detect and respond to potential ransomware threats in real-time. Use security tools, log analysis, and threat intelligence to proactively identify and address vulnerabilities.

Mitigating and removing ransomware requires a combination of technical measures, careful investigation, and remediation efforts. By identifying and quarantining infected systems, removing the ransomware, recovering from clean backups, and implementing security enhancements, organizations can effectively mitigate the impact of a ransomware attack. Ongoing monitoring, system scanning, employee education, and regular updates to the incident response plan are crucial for maintaining a robust defense against ransomware threats.

6.4 Data Recovery: Backup Restoration and File Decryption

Data recovery is a crucial aspect of ransomware incident response, as it allows organizations to regain access to encrypted or locked files without paying the ransom. This phase involves restoring data from secure backups and exploring decryption options when available. Here are key strategies for data recovery:

Assess Backup Availability and Integrity:

Determine the availability and integrity of backup data. Identify whether backups were properly maintained and secured. Ensure that backups were not compromised or affected by the ransomware attack.

Prioritize Critical Data Restoration:

Prioritize the restoration of critical data and systems that are essential for business operations. Consider the impact of data loss on the organization and prioritize the recovery of data based on business needs and recovery time objectives (RTOs).

Restore Data from Secure Backups:

Restore data from secure and verified backups. Ensure that the backup copies are clean and free from malware. Follow established backup restoration procedures and validate the integrity of restored data.

Test Restored Data and Systems:

Conduct thorough testing and verification of restored data and systems to ensure they are functioning as expected. Verify that the restored data is complete, accurate, and accessible. Test critical applications and services to confirm their proper functionality.

Explore File Decryption Options:

Research and explore available file decryption options. In some cases, security companies or law enforcement agencies may release decryption tools that can help recover files encrypted by specific ransomware variants. Check reputable sources and coordinate with incident response partners for decryption support.

Engage External Experts if Necessary:

If decryption options are limited or unavailable, consider engaging external experts or cybersecurity firms that specialize in ransomware analysis and decryption. These experts may have access to advanced tools and techniques that can help recover encrypted files.

Document Data Recovery Efforts:

Document all data recovery efforts, including the restoration process, decryption attempts, and any challenges encountered. This documentation serves as a record of the recovery process and aids in future incident analysis and reporting.

Strengthen Backup and Recovery Practices:

Evaluate and enhance backup and recovery practices based on lessons learned from the ransomware incident. Regularly review backup strategies, ensure backup copies are securely stored, and implement redundancy measures to minimize the impact of future attacks.

Educate Employees on Data Recovery Procedures:

Provide guidance to employees on the data recovery procedures they should follow if they encounter encrypted files or suspect a ransomware incident. Ensure employees are aware of the importance of promptly reporting such incidents to the incident response team.

Review and Update Business Continuity Plans:

Assess the effectiveness of business continuity plans and make necessary updates based on the lessons learned from the ransomware incident. Consider incorporating specific procedures for data recovery and restoration into the plans to ensure smooth operations during recovery.

Data recovery is a critical phase in ransomware incident response, allowing organizations to regain access to their encrypted files and systems. By assessing backup availability, prioritizing critical data restoration, exploring file decryption options, and engaging external experts if needed, organizations can successfully recover from a ransomware attack without paying the ransom. Documenting recovery efforts, strengthening backup practices, and updating business continuity plans contribute to improved preparedness and resilience against future ransomware incidents.

Chapter 7: Advanced Defense Techniques

As ransomware attacks continue to evolve in sophistication, organizations must stay one step ahead by employing advanced defense techniques. In this chapter, we will explore cutting-edge strategies and technologies that can enhance our ransomware defense capabilities. From leveraging artificial intelligence and machine learning to implementing behavior-based analysis and threat hunting, we will delve into advanced techniques that help detect and mitigate ransomware threats. By embracing these innovative approaches, we can strengthen our defenses and better protect our systems and data.

Section 7.1: Behavioral Analysis and Anomaly Detection

Behavioral analysis and anomaly detection provide valuable insights into the activities and patterns within our systems and networks. In this section, we will explore the use of behavior-based analysis to identify suspicious behaviors associated with ransomware attacks. We will discuss techniques such as user behavior analytics, network traffic analysis, and endpoint behavior monitoring. By leveraging these advanced methods, we can detect ransomware early and take proactive measures to mitigate its impact.

Section 7.2: Artificial Intelligence and Machine Learning

Artificial intelligence (AI) and machine learning (ML) have revolutionized the cybersecurity landscape, offering powerful tools for ransomware defense. In this section, we will discuss the applications of AI and ML in detecting and combating ransomware. We will explore the use of ML algorithms to analyze large datasets for identifying ransomware patterns and behaviors. Additionally, we will examine how AI-powered threat intelligence platforms can enhance our ability to detect and respond to ransomware attacks in real-time.

Section 7.3: Threat Hunting

Threat hunting involves actively searching for signs of malicious activity within our networks and systems. In this section, we will explore the concept of threat hunting and its application to ransomware defense. We will discuss techniques for proactively seeking out indicators of compromise (IOCs), analyzing logs and network data, and conducting targeted investigations. By adopting a proactive and iterative approach to threat hunting, we can identify and neutralize ransomware threats before they cause significant damage.

Section 7.4: Zero Trust Architecture

Zero Trust architecture is a security framework that assumes no inherent trust, even within our own networks. In this section, we will explore the principles of Zero Trust and its relevance to ransomware defense. We will discuss the implementation of strict access controls, multi-factor authentication, micro-segmentation, and continuous monitoring. By adopting a Zero Trust approach, we can minimize the attack surface, prevent lateral movement of ransomware, and limit the potential impact of an attack.

Advanced defense techniques are essential to combat the evolving threat landscape of ransomware. This chapter has explored the application of behavioral analysis and anomaly detection, artificial intelligence and machine learning, threat hunting, and Zero Trust architecture in ransomware defense. By leveraging these advanced techniques, organizations can gain deeper insights into ransomware attacks, detect threats more effectively, and respond swiftly to mitigate their impact.

As we progress through this book, we will continue to explore additional defense strategies and emerging technologies that further strengthen our ransomware defenses. By combining advanced defense techniques with a comprehensive security posture, we can stay resilient against the ever-changing ransomware landscape.

Let us now embrace the power of advanced defense techniques and elevate our ransomware defense capabilities. Together, we will build a robust defense that safeguards our systems, data, and organizational integrity.

7.1 Threat Intelligence and Proactive Monitoring

Threat intelligence and proactive monitoring are essential components of a comprehensive ransomware defense strategy. By staying informed about emerging threats, understanding attacker techniques, and actively monitoring network activity, organizations can detect and mitigate potential ransomware attacks before they cause significant damage. Here are key strategies for threat intelligence and proactive monitoring:

Establish a Threat Intelligence Program:

Develop a structured threat intelligence program that gathers, analyzes, and disseminates actionable intelligence about current and emerging ransomware threats. This program should include reliable sources such as industry reports, security vendors, government agencies, and information sharing communities.

Monitor Dark Web and Underground Forums:

Keep an eye on dark web marketplaces and underground forums where ransomware-as-a-service (RaaS) offerings, exploit kits, and stolen data may be traded. This monitoring can provide early indications of new ransomware variants, targeted industries, or potential attack vectors.

Subscribe to Security Alerts and Notifications:

Subscribe to security alerts and notifications from trusted sources, such as cybersecurity vendors, government agencies, and industry-specific information sharing platforms. These alerts can provide timely information about emerging ransomware threats and recommended mitigation strategies.

Conduct Regular Threat Assessments:

Perform regular assessments to identify and analyze the specific threats facing your organization. Assess the threat landscape, evaluate the potential impact of ransomware attacks, and identify vulnerabilities that could be exploited by threat actors.

Implement Security Information and Event Management (SIEM):

Deploy a robust Security Information and Event Management (SIEM) system to centralize and analyze log data from various sources. Implement real-time monitoring and correlation capabilities to identify potential indicators of compromise (IOCs) and detect anomalous behavior associated with ransomware attacks.

Employ Intrusion Detection and Prevention Systems (IDS/IPS):

Utilize intrusion detection and prevention systems (IDS/IPS) to monitor network traffic for known ransomware signatures and suspicious activities. Configure these systems to generate alerts or take automated actions to block or contain potential ransomware incidents.

Implement Endpoint Detection and Response (EDR) Solutions:

Deploy endpoint detection and response (EDR) solutions to monitor endpoints for suspicious behavior, file changes, and unauthorized processes associated with ransomware activity. Leverage the capabilities of EDR tools to detect and respond to potential ransomware incidents in real-time.

Conduct Regular Vulnerability Scans:

Perform regular vulnerability scans to identify weaknesses in systems, applications, and network infrastructure that could be exploited by ransomware attackers. Address identified vulnerabilities promptly through patching, configuration changes, or other mitigation measures.

Develop Security Baselines and Anomaly Detection:

Establish security baselines and develop anomaly detection mechanisms to identify deviations from normal network and system behavior. Monitor for unusual traffic patterns, communication with suspicious domains, or sudden spikes in file encryption activities that may indicate ransomware activity.

Collaborate with External Threat Intelligence Providers:

Engage with external threat intelligence providers and join industry-specific information sharing groups or alliances. Collaborate with peers, vendors, and law enforcement agencies to share intelligence, exchange insights, and collectively strengthen defenses against ransomware attacks.

Conduct Red Team Exercises and Penetration Testing:

Conduct red team exercises and penetration testing to simulate real-world ransomware attacks and identify potential security gaps. These proactive measures can help uncover vulnerabilities, validate security controls, and provide opportunities for remediation before actual attacks occur.

Stay Abreast of Security Research and Industry Trends:

Continuously educate yourself and your security team on the latest security research, industry trends, and best practices for ransomware defense. Attend conferences, webinars, and training sessions to stay updated and adapt your defense strategies accordingly.

Threat intelligence and proactive monitoring play a vital role in mitigating the risk of ransomware attacks. By establishing a threat intelligence program, monitoring dark web forums, subscribing to security alerts, conducting regular threat assessments, and leveraging security tools such as SIEM, IDS/IPS, and EDR, organizations can detect and respond to ransomware threats more effectively. Collaboration with external threat intelligence providers, vulnerability management, red team exercises, and staying informed about security research and industry trends further enhance an organization's ability to proactively defend against ransomware attacks.

7.2 Behavior-Based Detection and Machine Learning

Behavior-based detection and machine learning techniques are powerful tools in ransomware defense strategies. These approaches leverage advanced algorithms and analysis to identify patterns and anomalies indicative of ransomware activity. By focusing on the behavior of systems and users, organizations can detect and respond to ransomware attacks more effectively. Here are key strategies for behavior-based detection and machine learning in ransomware defense:

Collect and Analyze Behavioral Data:

Gather comprehensive behavioral data from various sources, including endpoints, network traffic, user activities, and system logs. This data serves as the foundation for building behavior profiles and identifying normal patterns of operation.

Establish Baseline Behavior:

Develop baseline behavior profiles for systems, users, and network traffic. These profiles capture normal behaviors, such as file access patterns, application usage, and network communication. Deviations from these baselines can indicate potential ransomware activity.

Use Machine Learning Algorithms:

Employ machine learning algorithms to analyze and model normal behaviors based on the collected data. These algorithms can identify subtle deviations, anomalies, or suspicious patterns that may indicate ransomware activity.

Train Models with Historical Data:

Train machine learning models using historical data that includes both normal and ransomware-related behaviors. This allows the models to learn from past incidents and improve their detection accuracy over time.

Monitor System and Network Behavior in Real-Time:

Continuously monitor system and network behavior in real-time using machine learning models. Analyze incoming data and compare it against established behavior profiles to detect deviations and potential ransomware activity.

Employ Endpoint Detection and Response (EDR) Solutions:

Deploy endpoint detection and response (EDR) solutions that leverage behavior-based detection.

These solutions monitor endpoint activities, detect suspicious behaviors, and generate alerts when ransomware-like behaviors are detected.

Implement Network Traffic Analysis Tools:

Utilize network traffic analysis tools that employ behavior-based detection to identify ransomware activity. Analyze network communications, protocol usage, and traffic patterns to detect anomalies and potential ransomware-related behaviors.

Incorporate User Behavior Analytics:

Integrate user behavior analytics (UBA) to detect abnormal user activities that may be indicative of ransomware attacks. UBA solutions can identify user behaviors that deviate from their established patterns, such as excessive file access or unusual login activities.

Leverage Threat Intelligence:

Combine behavior-based detection with threat intelligence to enhance detection capabilities. Integrate known ransomware indicators, signatures, and behavior patterns into detection algorithms to identify and block ransomware-related activities.

Continuously Update and Refine Models:

Regularly update and refine machine learning models to adapt to evolving ransomware tactics and techniques. Incorporate new data and feedback from detected incidents to improve the accuracy and effectiveness of behavior-based detection.

Conduct Regular Testing and Validation:

Conduct regular testing and validation of behavior-based detection systems to ensure their effectiveness. Use controlled test environments, threat simulations, and red team exercises to evaluate the detection capabilities and identify any limitations or false positives.

Integrate with Incident Response and Remediation:

Integrate behavior-based detection systems with incident response processes to enable swift action upon detection of ransomware activity. Automate response actions or generate alerts to initiate incident response procedures for containment, investigation, and remediation.

Behavior-based detection and machine learning techniques provide organizations with advanced capabilities to detect and respond to ransomware attacks. By analyzing behavioral data, establishing baseline behaviors, training machine learning models, and continuously monitoring system and network behavior, organizations can proactively identify ransomware activity. Integrating behavior-based detection with endpoint and network security solutions, user behavior analytics, and threat intelligence enhances detection accuracy. Regular testing, validation, and integration with incident response processes further strengthen an organization's ransomware defense capabilities.

7.3 Endpoint Detection and Response (EDR) Solutions

Endpoint Detection and Response (EDR) solutions play a critical role in ransomware defense strategies. These solutions provide real-time monitoring, threat detection, and incident response capabilities at the endpoint level, enabling organizations to quickly identify and mitigate ransomware threats. Here are key strategies for leveraging EDR solutions in ransomware defense:

Endpoint Visibility:

EDR solutions offer enhanced visibility into endpoints, providing organizations with detailed insights into the activities, processes, and behaviors occurring on individual devices. This visibility enables early detection of ransomware-related activities and suspicious behaviors.

Real-time Monitoring:

EDR solutions continuously monitor endpoint activity in real-time, analyzing various data sources such as process executions, file modifications, network connections, and system events. This monitoring allows for the timely detection of ransomware indicators and behavioral anomalies.

Behavior-based Threat Detection:

EDR solutions leverage behavior-based threat detection techniques to identify ransomware activity. By establishing baseline behaviors and employing machine learning algorithms, these solutions can detect deviations that may indicate the presence of ransomware.

Indicators of Compromise (IOCs):

EDR solutions maintain databases of known ransomware indicators of compromise (IOCs) such as file hashes, IP addresses, and domain names associated with known ransomware variants. By comparing endpoint activity against these IOCs, EDR solutions can quickly identify potential ransomware infections.

Threat Hunting:

EDR solutions enable proactive threat hunting, allowing security teams to search for signs of potential ransomware attacks across endpoints. By leveraging advanced search capabilities and data correlation, security professionals can uncover hidden threats and proactively respond to them.

Automated Response and Remediation:

EDR solutions offer automated response and remediation capabilities, allowing for the immediate containment and isolation of infected endpoints. Automated responses can include terminating malicious processes, quarantining files, or disconnecting compromised devices from the network to prevent further spread.

Incident Investigation and Forensics:

EDR solutions provide valuable insights for incident investigation and forensics. Security teams can analyze endpoint data captured by EDR solutions to understand the scope of the ransomware attack, trace the attack's origins, and identify potential entry points or vulnerabilities.

Integration with SIEM and Threat Intelligence:

Integrating EDR solutions with Security Information and Event Management (SIEM) systems and threat intelligence feeds enhances their effectiveness. This integration enables cross-correlation of endpoint data with network-wide security events and enriched threat intelligence, leading to more accurate and comprehensive threat detection.

User and Entity Behavior Analytics (UEBA):

Some advanced EDR solutions incorporate User and Entity Behavior Analytics (UEBA) capabilities to detect anomalous user activities and behaviors that may be indicative of ransomware attacks. UEBA analyzes user actions, account access patterns, and file interactions to identify suspicious activities.

Continuous Monitoring and Updates:

EDR solutions should be continuously monitored and updated to stay effective against evolving ransomware threats. Regularly applying vendor-provided updates and patches ensures that the solution can detect the latest ransomware variants and employ the most up-to-date threat detection techniques.

Employee Education and Awareness:

Educating employees about the role of EDR solutions and their importance in ransomware defense is crucial. Employees should be aware of EDR alerts, their significance, and the appropriate actions to take when an alert is triggered.

Ongoing EDR Solution Optimization:

Regularly assess and optimize the configuration and policies of EDR solutions to maximize their effectiveness. Fine-tuning detection rules, adjusting sensitivity levels, and incorporating lessons learned from incidents help improve the accuracy of ransomware detection and reduce false positives.

Endpoint Detection and Response (EDR) solutions provide organizations with crucial visibility, threat detection, and response capabilities at the endpoint level. By leveraging real-time monitoring, behavior-based detection, automated response, and integration with SIEM and threat intelligence, organizations can effectively detect and mitigate ransomware attacks. Continuous monitoring, employee education, and ongoing optimization of EDR solutions are vital for maintaining strong ransomware defense capabilities.

7.4 Data Encryption and Protection Mechanisms

Data encryption and protection mechanisms play a vital role in safeguarding sensitive information and mitigating the impact of ransomware attacks. By implementing strong encryption practices and adopting robust data protection strategies, organizations can minimize the risk of unauthorized access to their data. Here are key considerations for implementing data encryption and protection mechanisms in ransomware defense:

Encryption at Rest:

Implement encryption at rest to protect data stored in databases, file systems, and backup repositories. Encryption at rest ensures that even if attackers gain unauthorized access to the data, they cannot read or utilize it without the encryption keys.

Encryption in Transit:

Secure data transmissions by employing encryption in transit. Use protocols such as Transport Layer Security (TLS) or Secure Socket Layer (SSL) to encrypt data while it is being transmitted over networks, preventing interception and tampering by attackers.

Strong Authentication and Access Controls:

Implement strong authentication mechanisms, such as multi factor authentication (MFA), to ensure that only authorized users can access sensitive data. Additionally, enforce granular access controls based on the principle of least privilege, granting users access to only the data they need to perform their roles.

Data Classification and Segmentation:

Classify data based on its sensitivity and criticality. Segment networks and systems to create isolated environments that restrict access to sensitive data. By separating data into different segments, organizations can limit the impact of a ransomware attack and prevent lateral movement.

Backup Encryption:

Encrypt backups to protect against unauthorized access and ensure the confidentiality of sensitive data. Implement strong encryption mechanisms for both on-premises and cloud-based backups, and securely store encryption keys separate from the backed-up data.

Secure Key Management:

Establish robust key management practices to safeguard encryption keys. Implement secure key storage mechanisms, such as Hardware Security Modules (HSMs), and enforce strong access controls to prevent unauthorized access to encryption keys.

Data Loss Prevention (DLP) Solutions:

Deploy Data Loss Prevention (DLP) solutions to monitor and prevent unauthorized transmission or exfiltration of sensitive data. DLP solutions can detect and block attempts to send sensitive information outside the organization's network, adding an additional layer of protection against data breaches.

Regular Patching and Vulnerability Management:

Keep systems and software up to date with regular patching to address security vulnerabilities. Regularly scan and assess the network for vulnerabilities and promptly remediate any identified weaknesses to prevent attackers from exploiting them to gain unauthorized access.

Employee Training and Awareness:

Educate employees about the importance of data protection and encryption practices. Train them on recognizing phishing attempts, practicing secure password management, and handling sensitive information securely. Encourage a culture of security awareness and empower employees to be vigilant against potential ransomware threats.

Data Backup and Recovery:

Implement a comprehensive data backup and recovery strategy. Regularly back up critical data and verify the integrity of backups. Test the restoration process to ensure that data can be recovered successfully in the event of a ransomware attack.

Data Retention and Retraction:

Establish data retention and retraction policies to minimize the impact of a ransomware attack. Regularly review and delete unnecessary data, reducing the attack surface and potential impact of data loss.

Incident Response and Recovery Planning:

Develop and regularly test an incident response plan specific to ransomware attacks. This plan should outline the steps to be taken in the event of an attack, including data recovery procedures, communication protocols, and coordination with law enforcement and incident response teams.

Data encryption and protection mechanisms are crucial components of ransomware defense strategies. By implementing encryption at rest and in transit, enforcing strong authentication and access controls, classifying and segmenting data, and employing backup encryption and secure key management, organizations can significantly reduce the impact of ransomware attacks. Regular patching, employee training, and robust incident response planning further enhance data protection capabilities. By adopting these practices, organizations can better protect their sensitive information and minimize the risk of data breaches caused by ransomware attacks.

7.5 Deception Technologies: Honeypots and Honeytokens

Deception technologies, such as honeypots and honeytokens, play a crucial role in enhancing ransomware defense strategies. These technologies create attractive targets that lure attackers, divert their attention, and provide valuable insights into their tactics and techniques. Here's an overview of honeypots and honeytokens and their significance in ransomware defense:

Honeypots:

Honeypots are decoy systems or network components designed to mimic real assets within an organization's network. These systems appear as legitimate targets, attracting attackers and diverting their attention away from critical systems and data. Honeypots can be deployed at various levels, such as network-based, host-based, or application-based, depending on the organization's requirements.

Benefits of Honeypots:

- **Diversion of attackers**: Honeypots redirect attackers away from valuable assets, buying time for detection and response.
- **Early threat detection**: Honeypots allow organizations to capture and analyze the tactics, techniques, and tools used by attackers, providing valuable insights for threat intelligence.
- **Understanding attacker behavior**: Honeypots enable organizations to study and understand the techniques employed by attackers, enhancing incident response capabilities and strengthening overall defenses.
- **Alert generation**: Honeypots generate alerts when accessed, providing early warning signs of potential attacks.
- **Deceptive value**: Honeypots increase the attacker's effort and decrease their return on investment, discouraging future attacks.

Honeytokens:

Honeytokens are decoy data elements intentionally placed within an organization's systems, networks, or applications. These can be files, credentials, or other sensitive information that are not used by legitimate users. Honeytokens are designed to appear enticing to attackers and, when accessed, trigger an alarm indicating unauthorized access or compromise.

Benefits of Honeytokens:

- **Early detection of compromise**: Honeytokens provide a proactive mechanism for detecting unauthorized access or malicious activities within an organization's systems.
- **Indicative of specific attacks**: By strategically placing honeytokens across different systems or network segments, organizations can gain insights into the specific attack vectors and compromised areas.
- **Forensic analysis**: When a honeytoken is triggered, organizations can analyze the access logs and activities surrounding the event to gain valuable forensic information about the attack and the attacker's methods.
- **Increased security awareness**: Honeytokens raise security awareness among employees, encouraging vigilance and caution when accessing sensitive data or files.

Deployment Considerations:

When deploying honeypots and honeytokens, it is important to consider the following factors:

- **Proper segmentation**: Ensure that honeypots and honeytokens are deployed in isolated and controlled environments, separate from production systems and critical data.
- **Realistic configurations**: Configure honeypots to resemble actual assets, including

realistic vulnerabilities and services, to attract attackers.

- **Monitoring and logging**: Implement robust monitoring and logging mechanisms to capture and analyze activities within honeypots and honeytoken repositories.
- **Regular updates and maintenance**: Keep honeypots and honeytokens up to date with security patches and configurations to ensure their effectiveness and avoid being flagged as outdated or easily identifiable decoys.

Deception technologies, such as honeypots and honeytokens, are powerful tools in ransomware defense strategies. By diverting attackers, detecting threats early, and gaining insights into attacker behavior and techniques, organizations can enhance their overall security posture and better protect critical systems and data. Careful deployment and maintenance of honeypots and honeytokens enable organizations to proactively defend against ransomware attacks and gain valuable intelligence to strengthen their security defenses.

Chapter 8: Collaboration and Information Sharing

In the fight against ransomware, collaboration and information sharing are vital to staying ahead of evolving threats. In this chapter, we will explore the importance of collaborating with industry peers, sharing threat intelligence, and participating in information-sharing initiatives. By fostering a culture of collaboration and knowledge exchange, we can collectively enhance our ability to detect, prevent, and respond to ransomware attacks. In this chapter, we will delve into the benefits of collaboration, explore different platforms and initiatives, and discuss best practices for effective information sharing.

Section 8.1: Benefits of Collaboration

Collaboration brings numerous benefits to ransomware defense efforts. In this section, we will discuss the advantages of collaborating with industry peers, security vendors, and government agencies. We will explore how collaboration enables us to gain insights into emerging threats, share best practices, and pool resources to develop more effective defense strategies. By working together, we can create a stronger collective defense against ransomware.

Section 8.2: Sharing Threat Intelligence

Threat intelligence sharing plays a pivotal role in identifying and responding to ransomware threats. In this section, we will delve into the concept of threat intelligence and discuss the importance of sharing actionable information. We will explore different models of threat intelligence sharing, such as public-private partnerships, information sharing and analysis centers (ISACs), and sector-specific threat intelligence sharing communities. By participating in these initiatives, we can access timely and relevant threat intelligence to bolster our defenses.

Section 8.3: Collaborative Incident Response

Collaboration is essential during incident response, as ransomware attacks often have broader implications beyond a single organization. In this section, we will discuss the benefits of collaborative incident response efforts, such as sharing indicators of compromise (IOCs), analyzing attack techniques, and coordinating response actions. We will explore incident response platforms, forums, and communities that facilitate collaborative incident management. By working together, we can effectively contain and mitigate the impact of ransomware incidents.

Section 8.4: Best Practices for Information Sharing

To ensure effective information sharing, it is essential to follow best practices and adhere to relevant legal and ethical considerations. In this section, we will discuss guidelines for responsible information sharing, including anonymization of data, adherence to data privacy regulations, and establishing trust among participants. We will also explore platforms and frameworks that facilitate secure and controlled sharing of information. By following best practices, we can foster a culture of trust and collaboration while maintaining confidentiality and privacy.

Collaboration and information sharing are integral to combating the pervasive threat of ransomware. This chapter has highlighted the benefits of collaboration, the importance of sharing threat intelligence, the value of collaborative incident response, and best practices for responsible information sharing. By actively participating in collaborative initiatives, organizations can leverage collective knowledge and resources to strengthen their ransomware defenses.

As we continue our journey through this book, we will explore additional defense strategies and techniques to enhance our ransomware defense capabilities. By embracing collaboration and information sharing, we can build a united front against ransomware and protect our digital assets collectively.

Let us now embrace the power of collaboration and information sharing, joining forces to combat ransomware threats effectively. Together, we will create a resilient and interconnected defense ecosystem that safeguards our organizations and the broader community.

8.1 Engaging with Industry Peers and Security Communities

Engaging with industry peers and security communities is a crucial aspect of ransomware defense strategies. Collaboration and information sharing play a significant role in staying updated on the latest threats, trends, and mitigation techniques. By actively participating in industry forums, conferences, and security communities, organizations can gain valuable insights, build networks, and strengthen their defense against ransomware. Here are the key benefits and strategies for engaging with industry peers and security communities:

Information Exchange:

Engaging with industry peers and security communities allows for the exchange of information regarding emerging threats, attack techniques, and best practices. By participating in discussions and sharing experiences, organizations can learn from others' challenges and successes, helping them stay informed and proactive in their defense against ransomware.

Early Warning System:

Industry peers and security communities often act as an early warning system, providing alerts and notifications about new ransomware campaigns, vulnerabilities, and indicators of compromise. This timely information can help organizations take proactive measures to mitigate risks and prevent attacks.

Threat Intelligence Sharing:

Collaborating with industry peers and security communities enables the sharing of threat intelligence, such as indicators of compromise (IOCs), malware samples, and attack patterns. This shared intelligence can enhance the detection and response capabilities of organizations, allowing them to identify and block ransomware threats more effectively.

Peer Learning and Benchmarking:

Engaging with industry peers provides opportunities for peer learning and benchmarking. By understanding how other organizations approach ransomware defense and learning from their strategies, organizations can identify gaps in their own security posture and adopt best practices to strengthen their defenses.

Collaboration on Research and Development:

Security communities often foster collaboration on research and development efforts. By participating in joint initiatives, organizations can contribute to the development of new technologies, tools, and techniques aimed at combating ransomware. This collaborative approach accelerates the innovation and effectiveness of defense strategies.

Sharing Incident Response and Recovery Experiences:

Engaging with industry peers and security communities allows organizations to share their incident response and recovery experiences. This sharing of real-world scenarios and lessons learned enables others to understand effective mitigation strategies, improve incident response plans, and enhance their overall resilience against ransomware attacks.

Participation in Security Events and Conferences:

Actively participating in security events, conferences, and webinars provides opportunities to learn from experts, attend informative sessions, and engage in discussions with industry leaders. These events often feature presentations and workshops on ransomware defense strategies, threat intelligence, and emerging technologies, enabling organizations to stay abreast of the latest trends and solutions.

Joining Information Sharing Platforms:

Organizations can join information sharing platforms and security communities that facilitate the exchange of threat intelligence and collaboration among members. These platforms enable real-time sharing of threat data, analysis of new ransomware variants, and discussions on effective defense strategies.

Contributing to Vulnerability Disclosure and Responsible Disclosure Programs:

By actively participating in vulnerability disclosure and responsible disclosure programs, organizations can contribute to the overall security of the industry. Reporting vulnerabilities responsibly and sharing findings with relevant parties helps in the timely patching of vulnerabilities and reduces the potential for ransomware attacks.

Engaging with industry peers and security communities is a valuable and essential component of ransomware defense strategies. Through information exchange, threat intelligence sharing, peer learning, and collaboration on research and development, organizations can enhance their knowledge, detection capabilities, and incident response efforts. By actively participating in security events, joining information sharing platforms, and contributing to responsible disclosure programs, organizations demonstrate their commitment to collective security and strengthen the resilience of the entire industry against ransomware attacks.

8.2 Sharing Threat Intelligence and Best Practices

Sharing threat intelligence and best practices is a crucial aspect of ransomware defense strategies. By collaborating and exchanging information with trusted partners, organizations can strengthen their collective defenses and stay ahead of evolving ransomware threats. Here are the key benefits and strategies for sharing threat intelligence and best practices:

Early Detection and Response:

Sharing threat intelligence enables early detection of emerging ransomware threats. By exchanging information about new attack techniques, indicators of compromise (IOCs), and malware samples, organizations can proactively identify and block ransomware attacks before they cause significant damage. Rapid response and mitigation measures can be implemented based on the shared intelligence, reducing the impact of attacks.

Collective Defense:

Sharing threat intelligence and best practices fosters a collective defense approach. By collaborating with trusted partners, industry peers, and security communities, organizations can pool their knowledge and resources to create a more robust defense ecosystem. This collaborative effort helps in identifying common attack patterns, sharing insights into attacker behavior, and collectively developing effective countermeasures against ransomware.

Enhancing Detection Capabilities:

Shared threat intelligence can improve detection capabilities. By analyzing and incorporating shared IOCs and indicators of compromise into security systems, organizations can enhance their ability to detect and block ransomware attacks. This shared intelligence acts as an additional layer of defense, providing early warning signs and improving overall security posture.

Incident Response Improvement:

Sharing best practices and lessons learned from ransomware incidents helps organizations improve their incident response capabilities. By understanding how others have successfully handled ransomware attacks, organizations can enhance their own response plans, develop effective containment strategies, and streamline recovery processes.

Sharing incident response experiences also helps identify common pitfalls and mitigation techniques.

Cross-Industry Collaboration:

Collaborating with organizations from different industries and sectors facilitates a broader perspective on ransomware threats. Sharing threat intelligence and best practices across industries allows organizations to gain insights into unique attack vectors, discover new mitigation techniques, and learn from diverse approaches to ransomware defense. This cross-industry collaboration strengthens overall defenses and helps address the evolving nature of ransomware attacks.

Trusted Sharing Networks and Platforms:

Organizations can participate in trusted sharing networks and platforms specifically designed for sharing threat intelligence and best practices. These platforms provide secure environments for exchanging sensitive information, facilitating real-time communication, and allowing for rapid response to emerging threats. Trusted networks and platforms ensure confidentiality, authenticity, and integrity of shared information.

Information Sharing Agreements:

Establishing information sharing agreements and partnerships with trusted organizations enables the exchange of threat intelligence. These agreements define the terms, scope, and methods of sharing, ensuring that both parties benefit from the collaboration. Information sharing agreements can involve formal partnerships, industry-specific information sharing groups, or ad-hoc collaborations based on mutual trust and shared objectives.

Anonymized Data Sharing:

In cases where organizations may be concerned about sharing sensitive information, anonymized data sharing can be an option. By removing personally identifiable information (PII) and other sensitive data from threat intelligence, organizations can share valuable insights and trends without compromising privacy or confidentiality. Anonymized data sharing allows for the exchange of valuable intelligence while maintaining data protection and compliance.

Government and Law Enforcement Collaboration:

Collaboration with government agencies and law enforcement entities is essential for sharing threat intelligence related to ransomware attacks. Public-private partnerships enable organizations to share information securely with relevant authorities, facilitating coordinated responses, investigations, and the identification of threat actors. Close collaboration with government and law enforcement entities strengthens the collective fight against ransomware.

Sharing threat intelligence and best practices is critical for effective ransomware defense. By collaborating with trusted partners, participating in information sharing networks, and establishing information sharing agreements, organizations can enhance their detection capabilities, improve incident response, and strengthen their collective defenses against ransomware. Sharing threat intelligence not only helps in early detection and response but also facilitates cross-industry collaboration and fosters a proactive and collaborative approach to tackling ransomware threats. Through these efforts, organizations can collectively stay ahead of evolving ransomware attacks and better protect their critical assets and data.

8.3 Collaborating with Law Enforcement and Cybersecurity Organizations

Collaborating with law enforcement and cybersecurity organizations is a crucial component of effective ransomware defense strategies. By partnering with these entities, organizations can leverage their expertise, resources, and legal authority to enhance their defenses, investigate attacks, and apprehend threat actors. Here are the key benefits and strategies for collaborating with law enforcement and cybersecurity organizations:

Access to Specialized Expertise:

Law enforcement and cybersecurity organizations have specialized knowledge and expertise in dealing with cybercrime, including ransomware attacks. Collaborating with these entities provides organizations with access to seasoned professionals who can offer valuable guidance, investigative support, and technical assistance to mitigate ransomware threats effectively.

Legal and Regulatory Support:

Law enforcement agencies have the legal authority to investigate and prosecute cybercriminals involved in ransomware attacks. Collaborating with law enforcement ensures that attacks are reported and proper legal procedures are followed. By working together, organizations can benefit from the legal and regulatory support provided by law enforcement entities, increasing the chances of successful prosecution and deterrence of future attacks.

Incident Response Coordination:

Collaborating with law enforcement and cybersecurity organizations facilitates coordinated incident response efforts. When a ransomware attack occurs, these entities can provide guidance on proper incident handling procedures, evidence preservation, and the collection of actionable intelligence. This coordination ensures a more effective and streamlined response, minimizing the impact of the attack and maximizing the chances of successful recovery.

Threat Intelligence Sharing:

Law enforcement and cybersecurity organizations have access to extensive threat intelligence networks and databases. Collaborating with these entities enables organizations to receive timely and relevant threat intelligence related to ransomware attacks. This shared intelligence includes indicators of compromise (IOCs), attack trends, and information on threat actors. Leveraging this threat intelligence enhances an organization's ability to detect, prevent, and respond to ransomware attacks.

Joint Training and Exercises:

Collaborative efforts with law enforcement and cybersecurity organizations provide opportunities for joint training and exercises. Organizations can participate in workshops, tabletop exercises, and simulated attack scenarios conducted by these entities. This training enhances the organization's readiness to handle ransomware incidents, improves incident response capabilities, and strengthens overall resilience.

Reporting and Information Sharing:

Collaborating with law enforcement entities ensures that ransomware attacks are properly reported and documented. Reporting attacks to law enforcement agencies assists in the investigation process and contributes to the collective understanding of the ransomware threat landscape. Additionally, sharing information and insights gained from attacks with law enforcement and cybersecurity organizations helps in building a comprehensive knowledge base for identifying and prosecuting threat actors.

Public-Private Partnerships:

Public-private partnerships play a crucial role in combating ransomware attacks. Collaborating with law enforcement and cybersecurity organizations in public-private initiatives strengthens the collective response to ransomware threats. These partnerships foster information sharing, joint research and development, and the development of effective strategies to combat ransomware. Public-private partnerships also enable organizations to contribute to policy discussions and advocacy efforts aimed at addressing the root causes of ransomware attacks.

Trust and Confidentiality:

Collaborating with law enforcement and cybersecurity organizations requires establishing trust and ensuring confidentiality. Organizations should work with trusted partners who prioritize data protection, confidentiality, and compliance with legal and regulatory requirements. Clear communication channels and agreements should be established to maintain the confidentiality of sensitive information shared during collaboration.

Collaborating with law enforcement and cybersecurity organizations is instrumental in combating ransomware attacks. By accessing specialized expertise, leveraging legal and regulatory support, coordinating incident response, sharing threat intelligence, and participating in joint training and exercises, organizations can enhance their defense capabilities and increase the chances of successful prosecution of threat actors. Public-private partnerships and trust-building efforts contribute to a collective and coordinated response to the ransomware threat, ultimately making the digital landscape safer for organizations and individuals alike.

Chapter 9: Compliance and Regulatory Considerations

Compliance with relevant regulations and adherence to industry standards are crucial components of an effective ransomware defense strategy. In this chapter, we will explore the importance of compliance and regulatory considerations in protecting against ransomware attacks. We will delve into key compliance frameworks, industry-specific regulations, and best practices for ensuring security and privacy in the face of ransomware threats. By understanding and implementing compliance requirements, organizations can mitigate risks, avoid penalties, and establish a strong security foundation.

Section 9.1: Compliance Frameworks and Standards

Compliance frameworks provide organizations with guidelines and best practices for establishing robust security controls. In this section, we will discuss prominent compliance frameworks, such as the Payment Card Industry Data Security Standard (PCI DSS), the General Data Protection Regulation (GDPR), and the Health Insurance Portability and Accountability Act (HIPAA). We will explore the specific requirements of these frameworks and how they address ransomware defense. By aligning with relevant compliance frameworks, organizations can ensure a strong security posture that protects against ransomware threats.

Section 9.2: Industry-Specific Regulations

Many industries have specific regulations and requirements aimed at safeguarding sensitive data and critical infrastructure. In this section, we will explore industry-specific regulations, such as the financial sector's Sarbanes-Oxley Act (SOX) and the energy sector's North American Electric Reliability Corporation Critical Infrastructure Protection (NERC CIP) standards. We will discuss how these regulations address ransomware defense and the additional measures organizations in these industries should consider. By understanding and complying with industry-specific regulations, organizations can meet the unique challenges posed by ransomware attacks.

Section 9.3: Data Protection and Privacy

Data protection and privacy regulations play a significant role in ransomware defense. In this section, we will explore the impact of regulations like the GDPR, the California Consumer Privacy Act (CCPA), and other global data protection laws on ransomware defense strategies. We will discuss the importance of implementing strong data protection measures, conducting privacy impact assessments, and ensuring secure data handling practices. By prioritizing data protection and privacy, organizations can safeguard sensitive information from ransomware attacks and maintain customer trust.

Section 9.4: Incident Reporting and Compliance

Prompt and accurate incident reporting is often a requirement under various compliance regulations. In this section, we will discuss the importance of incident reporting in the context of ransomware attacks. We will explore reporting obligations under different regulations and discuss best practices for incident documentation, communication, and coordination with regulatory bodies. By adhering to incident reporting requirements, organizations can fulfill their compliance obligations and contribute to a collective understanding of ransomware threats.

Compliance with regulations and adherence to industry standards are integral to an effective ransomware defense strategy. This chapter has highlighted the significance of compliance frameworks and industry-specific regulations, as well as the importance of data protection and privacy considerations. We have also discussed the role of incident reporting in maintaining compliance obligations. By prioritizing compliance and regulatory considerations, organizations can build a strong foundation for ransomware defense and demonstrate their commitment to security and privacy.

As we continue our exploration of ransomware defense strategies in this book, we will delve into additional techniques and best practices. By combining compliance and regulatory considerations with technical measures and a comprehensive security approach, we can establish a resilient defense against ransomware and protect our valuable assets.

Let us now embrace compliance and regulatory requirements, integrating them into our ransomware defense strategy. Together, we will navigate the regulatory landscape, mitigate risks, and safeguard our organizations from the devastating impact of ransomware attacks.

9.1 Overview of Data Protection Regulations and Standards

Data protection regulations and standards play a critical role in safeguarding sensitive information and ensuring privacy in an increasingly digital world. Organizations must understand and comply with these regulations to protect their data from unauthorized access, loss, or misuse. In this chapter, we will provide an overview of some key data protection regulations and standards that are relevant to ransomware defense strategies.

General Data Protection Regulation (GDPR):

The GDPR is a comprehensive data protection regulation implemented by the European Union (EU) in 2018. It sets forth strict requirements for the collection, storage, and processing of personal data of EU citizens. The GDPR establishes principles such as data minimization, purpose limitation, and the right to erasure, empowering individuals to have control over their personal information. Compliance with the GDPR is essential for organizations that handle EU citizens' data, regardless of their geographic location.

California Consumer Privacy Act (CCPA):

The CCPA is a data protection law enacted in the state of California, United States. It grants consumers certain rights regarding their personal information, such as the right to know what data is collected, the right to opt-out of data sharing, and the right to request the deletion of their data. The CCPA applies to businesses that collect and process personal information of California residents and meet certain revenue or data processing thresholds.

Health Insurance Portability and Accountability Act (HIPAA):

HIPAA is a U.S. law that establishes standards for the protection of individuals' health information. It applies to healthcare providers, health plans, and healthcare clearinghouses, as well as their business associates. HIPAA requires organizations to implement safeguards to protect electronic protected health information (ePHI) from unauthorized access, disclosure, and alteration. Compliance with HIPAA is crucial for organizations in the healthcare industry.

Payment Card Industry Data Security Standard (PCI DSS):

The PCI DSS is a set of security standards developed by major credit card companies to protect cardholder data. It applies to organizations that handle, process, or store payment card information. PCI DSS outlines requirements for maintaining a secure network, implementing strong access controls, regularly monitoring and testing security systems, and maintaining an information security policy. Compliance with PCI DSS helps mitigate the risk of payment card data breaches.

ISO/IEC 27001:

ISO/IEC 27001 is an internationally recognized standard for information security management systems (ISMS). It provides a framework for organizations to establish, implement, maintain, and continually improve an ISMS, ensuring the confidentiality, integrity, and availability of information. ISO/IEC 27001 covers a broad range of security controls and risk management practices, making it a valuable standard for organizations seeking to enhance their overall data protection posture.

NIST Cybersecurity Framework:

The NIST Cybersecurity Framework, developed by the National Institute of Standards and Technology (NIST) in the United States, provides guidelines and best practices for managing cybersecurity risks. It offers a flexible framework that can be adapted to various organizations and sectors. The framework consists of five core functions: Identify, Protect, Detect, Respond, and Recover, which help organizations align their cybersecurity efforts and develop a proactive approach to data protection.

Data Breach Notification Laws:

Many jurisdictions have data breach notification laws that require organizations to notify affected individuals and authorities in the event of a data breach. These laws typically outline specific timeframes and requirements for reporting breaches, aiming to promote transparency and enable individuals to take necessary actions to protect themselves from potential harm.

Compliance with data protection regulations and standards is essential for organizations to protect sensitive data, maintain customer trust, and avoid legal and financial consequences. Understanding the requirements of these regulations and implementing appropriate security measures is a crucial aspect of ransomware defense strategies. In the following chapters, we will delve deeper into specific considerations and practices to ensure compliance with data protection regulations while defending against ransomware attacks.

9.2 Incorporating Compliance Requirements into Ransomware Defense

Compliance with data protection regulations is not only a legal obligation but also an essential aspect of a robust ransomware defense strategy. By aligning your defense measures with compliance requirements, you can enhance your organization's security posture and mitigate the risk of ransomware attacks. In this chapter, we will explore how to incorporate compliance requirements into your ransomware defense efforts effectively.

Understand the Regulatory Landscape:

Begin by gaining a comprehensive understanding of the data protection regulations applicable to your organization. Familiarize yourself with the specific requirements and obligations outlined in regulations such as the GDPR, CCPA, HIPAA, PCI DSS, ISO/IEC

27001, and any other relevant regulations. Stay updated on changes and amendments to these regulations to ensure ongoing compliance.

Conduct a Compliance Gap Analysis:

Perform a thorough assessment of your current security practices and compare them against the requirements specified in the applicable regulations. Identify any gaps or areas where your organization may fall short of compliance. This gap analysis will provide insights into the specific compliance measures that need to be implemented or strengthened within your ransomware defense strategy.

Integrate Privacy by Design:

Privacy by Design is a principle that emphasizes the proactive integration of privacy measures throughout the entire lifecycle of data processing activities. Incorporate Privacy by Design principles into your ransomware defense strategy by considering privacy implications when designing and implementing security controls. This includes practices such as data minimization, purpose limitation, and implementing privacy-enhancing technologies.

Implement Access Controls and User Permissions:

Compliance regulations often require organizations to enforce strict access controls and user permissions. Ensure that you have robust authentication mechanisms in place, such as strong passwords, multi-factor authentication, and least privilege access. Regularly review and update user permissions to align with the principle of least privilege, granting users only the necessary access required to perform their job functions.

Encrypt Sensitive Data:

Data encryption is a fundamental security measure that helps protect sensitive information from unauthorized access or disclosure. Implement encryption techniques to secure data both at rest and in transit. Encrypting data minimizes the impact of a ransomware attack by making it more difficult for threat actors to access and exploit the encrypted information.

Conduct Regular Risk Assessments and Audits:

Regular risk assessments and audits are crucial for maintaining compliance and identifying potential vulnerabilities in your security infrastructure. Perform risk assessments to identify areas of weakness and prioritize remediation efforts. Conduct internal or external audits to validate your compliance efforts and ensure adherence to the applicable regulations.

Implement Incident Response and Reporting Procedures:

Compliance regulations often require organizations to have incident response and reporting procedures in place. Establish a robust incident response plan that outlines the steps to be taken in the event of a ransomware attack. Ensure that your plan includes clear reporting mechanisms to promptly notify the appropriate regulatory authorities and affected individuals, as required by the applicable regulations.

Train Employees on Compliance and Security:

Employee training is essential for creating a culture of compliance and security awareness within your organization. Conduct regular training sessions to educate employees about data protection regulations, security best practices, and the risks associated with ransomware attacks. Emphasize the importance of compliance and provide guidance on how employees can contribute to maintaining a secure environment.

Engage with Compliance Experts:

Consider seeking guidance from compliance experts or consultants who specialize in data protection regulations. They can provide valuable insights, assist in conducting compliance assessments, and offer recommendations tailored to your organization's specific needs and regulatory requirements.

Monitor and Update Compliance Measures:

Compliance requirements evolve over time, and it is crucial to monitor and update your ransomware defense strategy accordingly. Stay informed about changes in regulations and industry best practices, and adapt your security measures to align with the latest compliance requirements. Regularly review and update your policies, procedures, and security controls to ensure ongoing compliance.

By incorporating compliance requirements into your ransomware defense strategy, you establish a strong foundation for protecting sensitive data, maintaining regulatory compliance, and effectively mitigating the risk of ransomware attacks. Remember that compliance is an ongoing process that requires continuous monitoring, improvement, and adaptation to keep pace with the evolving threat landscape and regulatory changes.

9.3 Security Frameworks: NIST Cybersecurity Framework, ISO 27001, etc.

Security frameworks provide organizations with structured guidelines and best practices for establishing effective cybersecurity and data protection measures. They offer a systematic approach to managing risks, enhancing security controls, and achieving regulatory compliance. In this chapter, we will explore some widely recognized security frameworks, including the NIST Cybersecurity Framework and ISO 27001, and discuss how they can be leveraged to strengthen ransomware defense strategies.

NIST Cybersecurity Framework:

The NIST Cybersecurity Framework, developed by the National Institute of Standards and Technology (NIST), is a widely adopted framework for improving cybersecurity risk management. It provides a flexible and scalable approach to managing cybersecurity risks and aligning organizational practices with business objectives. The framework consists of five core functions: Identify, Protect, Detect, Respond, and Recover. Each function includes categories and subcategories that guide organizations in implementing specific security controls and practices.

- **Identify**: Understand and manage cybersecurity risks to systems, assets, data, and capabilities.
- **Protect**: Implement safeguards to protect against potential cyber threats.
- **Detect**: Establish capabilities to identify cybersecurity events promptly.

- **Respond**: Develop and implement an effective incident response plan.
- **Recover**: Restore normal operations and minimize the impact of cybersecurity incidents.

Organizations can use the NIST Cybersecurity Framework to assess their current security posture, identify gaps, and prioritize actions to strengthen their ransomware defense strategies.

ISO/IEC 27001:

ISO/IEC 27001 is an internationally recognized standard for information security management systems (ISMS). It provides a systematic approach to managing sensitive information, ensuring its confidentiality, integrity, and availability. ISO 27001 outlines a comprehensive set of controls and risk management practices, allowing organizations to establish and maintain a robust security framework. It covers areas such as risk assessment, security policy development, asset management, access control, incident management, and business continuity planning.

Implementing ISO 27001 helps organizations establish a structured framework for protecting their critical information assets, including defense against ransomware attacks. It involves conducting risk assessments, implementing appropriate security controls, defining security policies and procedures, and establishing a culture of continuous improvement.

CIS Controls:

The Center for Internet Security (CIS) Controls is a widely recognized framework for implementing cybersecurity best practices. It provides a prioritized list of 20 critical security controls that organizations can adopt to improve their cybersecurity posture. The controls encompass various areas, including inventory and control of hardware and software assets, continuous vulnerability management, secure configuration of systems, controlled use of administrative privileges, data recovery capabilities, and security awareness training for employees.

By implementing the CIS Controls, organizations can address common security vulnerabilities and enhance their defenses against ransomware attacks.

Payment Card Industry Data Security Standard (PCI DSS):

While primarily focused on payment card data security, the PCI DSS provides a comprehensive framework for protecting sensitive cardholder information. It includes requirements for maintaining a secure network, implementing strong access controls, regularly monitoring and testing security systems, and maintaining an information security policy.

Compliance with PCI DSS is crucial for organizations handling payment card data and helps mitigate the risk of payment card data breaches, including ransomware attacks targeting payment systems.

Industry-Specific Frameworks:

Certain industries have established their own security frameworks tailored to their specific needs and regulatory requirements. For example, the healthcare industry has the Health Information Trust Alliance (HITRUST) Common Security Framework, which integrates various regulations, standards, and best practices to protect electronic health information. Similarly, the financial industry has the FFIEC Cybersecurity Assessment Tool, developed by the Federal Financial Institutions Examination Council, to assist financial institutions in assessing their cybersecurity risks and defenses.

Organizations operating in specific industries should consider adopting industry-specific frameworks in addition to general frameworks to ensure compliance with sector-specific regulations and standards.

By leveraging these security frameworks, organizations can establish a solid foundation for their ransomware defense strategies. These frameworks provide comprehensive guidance, best practices, and controls that organizations can implement to protect their sensitive data, detect and respond to ransomware attacks, and maintain regulatory compliance. It is important to tailor the implementation of these frameworks to the specific needs and risk profile of each organization while considering industry-specific requirements. Regular reviews, updates, and audits are necessary to ensure continued adherence to the frameworks and to keep pace with the evolving threat landscape.

Chapter 10: Future Trends and Emerging Technologies

The landscape of ransomware threats is ever-evolving, and staying ahead requires a keen eye on future trends and emerging technologies. In this final chapter, we will explore the potential future developments in ransomware attacks and the technologies that hold promise for defending against them. By understanding these trends and embracing emerging technologies, organizations can prepare themselves to tackle the challenges of tomorrow's ransomware landscape.

Section 10.1: Ransomware Trends and Evolution

Ransomware attacks continue to adapt and evolve, posing new challenges for defenders. In this section, we will discuss the emerging trends in ransomware, such as fileless ransomware, targeted attacks on critical infrastructure, and the rise of ransomware-as-a-service (RaaS) models. We will explore the motivations and tactics of attackers and how they are likely to shape the future threat landscape. By understanding these trends, organizations can proactively adapt their defense strategies to mitigate emerging threats.

Section 10.2: Artificial Intelligence in Ransomware Defense

Artificial intelligence (AI) has the potential to revolutionize ransomware defense by augmenting human capabilities and improving threat detection and response. In this section, we will explore the role of AI in ransomware defense, including the use of machine learning algorithms for anomaly detection, behavioral analysis, and predictive analytics. We will discuss the benefits and challenges of integrating AI into existing defense strategies and how it can enhance our ability to detect and mitigate ransomware threats.

Section 10.3: Blockchain and Distributed Ledger Technology

Blockchain and distributed ledger technology (DLT) offer new possibilities for securing data and preventing unauthorized modifications. In this section, we will explore the potential applications of blockchain and DLT in ransomware defense. We will discuss the use of blockchain for securing backups, ensuring data integrity, and establishing trust in multi-party collaborations. By leveraging the inherent security features of blockchain and DLT, organizations can mitigate the risk of ransomware attacks and enhance data protection.

Section 10.4: Cyber Threat Intelligence Platforms

Cyber threat intelligence platforms provide organizations with actionable insights into emerging threats and attack trends. In this section, we will explore the capabilities of threat intelligence platforms and their role in ransomware defense. We will discuss how these platforms aggregate and analyze data from various sources to provide real-time threat intelligence and support proactive defense measures. By leveraging cyber threat intelligence platforms, organizations can gain a deeper understanding of ransomware threats and strengthen their defense posture.

In this final chapter, we have explored future trends and emerging technologies in ransomware defense. We discussed the evolving nature of ransomware attacks and the need for organizations to stay vigilant and adaptive. We also examined the potential of artificial intelligence, blockchain and distributed ledger technology, and cyber threat intelligence platforms in enhancing ransomware defense capabilities.

As the threat landscape continues to evolve, it is crucial for organizations to remain proactive and informed. By keeping abreast of emerging trends and embracing innovative technologies, we can fortify our defenses and effectively combat ransomware attacks.

Let us now embark on a journey of continuous learning and adaptation, embracing the future of ransomware defense. Together, we can navigate the ever-changing threat landscape, safeguard our digital assets, and protect our organizations from the disruptive and damaging effects of ransomware attacks.

10.1 Evolving Landscape of Ransomware Attacks: Ransomware-as-a-Service (RaaS), AI-driven attacks, etc.

The threat landscape of ransomware attacks is constantly evolving, with threat actors adopting new techniques and exploiting emerging technologies to maximize their impact. In this chapter, we will explore some of the emerging trends and advancements in ransomware attacks, including Ransomware-as-a-Service (RaaS), AI-driven attacks, and other notable developments.

Ransomware-as-a-Service (RaaS):

Ransomware-as-a-Service has gained prominence in recent years, allowing even novice cybercriminals to launch ransomware attacks. RaaS platforms provide a user-friendly interface and infrastructure, enabling individuals or groups to distribute ransomware in exchange for a share of the ransom payments. RaaS lowers the entry barrier for cybercriminals and contributes to the proliferation of ransomware attacks. It is crucial to understand the workings of RaaS and its associated risks to develop effective defense strategies.

AI-driven Ransomware:

Artificial intelligence (AI) and machine learning (ML) techniques are being increasingly employed by both attackers and defenders. Cybercriminals leverage AI algorithms to enhance the sophistication and evasion capabilities of their ransomware attacks. They can automate tasks such as target selection, phishing campaigns, and even adjusting the ransom amount based on the victim's ability to pay. AI-driven ransomware poses a significant challenge for traditional security measures and requires advanced defense strategies that incorporate AI-powered detection and response mechanisms.

Double Extortion:

Double extortion is a tactic employed by ransomware operators to increase their chances of financial gain. In addition to encrypting victim's files, attackers exfiltrate sensitive data before encrypting it, threatening to publicly release or sell the stolen information if the ransom demands are not met. Double extortion adds an extra layer of pressure on victims, as they not only face the loss of their data but also the potential reputational and legal consequences of data leakage. Defending against double extortion requires a combination of robust backup strategies, data protection measures, and incident response plans.

Targeting of Critical Infrastructure:

Ransomware attacks have increasingly targeted critical infrastructure sectors such as healthcare, energy, transportation, and government institutions. Disrupting essential services can have severe consequences, posing risks to public safety, economic stability, and national security. Protecting critical infrastructure requires a multi-layered defense approach, including threat intelligence sharing, enhanced security measures, and close collaboration between public and private sector entities.

Mobile Ransomware:

With the proliferation of smartphones and mobile devices, cybercriminals have expanded their focus to mobile ransomware. Mobile ransomware can infect devices through malicious apps, compromised websites, or phishing attacks, locking users out of their devices or encrypting their data. Mobile ransomware poses unique challenges due to the diverse mobile operating systems and app ecosystems. Implementing mobile device management (MDM) solutions, educating users about mobile security best practices, and leveraging mobile security tools can help mitigate the risks associated with mobile ransomware.

Fileless Ransomware:

Fileless ransomware attacks exploit vulnerabilities in software and use legitimate system tools to execute malicious code directly in memory, without leaving traces on the hard drive. This makes detection and removal challenging for traditional security solutions. Fileless ransomware attacks often rely on exploiting vulnerabilities in software or using social engineering techniques to gain initial access. Robust patch management, secure configurations, and advanced endpoint protection solutions are crucial in combating fileless ransomware.

Dark Web Marketplaces and Cryptocurrency:

The use of cryptocurrencies, such as Bitcoin, has facilitated the anonymity and ease of ransom payments for cybercriminals. Dark web marketplaces provide platforms for ransomware operators to sell their ransomware variants, tools, and services, further fueling the ransomware ecosystem. Understanding the role of cryptocurrencies and the dark web in ransomware attacks is important for developing effective countermeasures and collaborating with law enforcement agencies.

As ransomware attacks continue to evolve, organizations must stay vigilant, adapt their defense strategies, and leverage advanced technologies to detect, prevent, and respond to these evolving threats. Implementing a proactive and multi-layered defense approach, including employee education, advanced threat detection, incident response planning, and collaboration with industry peers, is essential in combating the evolving landscape of ransomware attacks.

10.2 Role of Artificial Intelligence and Machine Learning in Ransomware Defense

Artificial Intelligence (AI) and Machine Learning (ML) have emerged as powerful technologies in the field of cybersecurity, including ransomware defense. These advanced techniques offer the potential to detect, prevent, and respond to ransomware attacks more effectively. In this chapter, we will explore the role of AI and ML in ransomware defense and how they can enhance organizations' security posture.

Threat Detection and Prevention:

AI and ML algorithms can analyze vast amounts of data, identify patterns, and detect anomalies associated with ransomware attacks. By leveraging historical data and continuously learning from new threats, AI-powered systems can identify potential indicators of ransomware activity, such as unusual network traffic, file behavior, or system changes. These technologies can enable early detection and proactive prevention of ransomware attacks, reducing the risk of successful infiltration.

Behavioral Analysis:

AI and ML algorithms can analyze user and system behavior to establish baseline patterns and detect deviations that may indicate ransomware activity. By monitoring file access patterns, application behaviors, and user interactions, AI-driven systems can identify suspicious activities and trigger alerts or automated responses. Behavioral analysis can help detect ransomware attacks that attempt to evade signature-based detection methods.

Malware Classification and Variants Detection:

Ransomware attacks often involve the use of different malware variants and rapidly evolving techniques. AI and ML can analyze ransomware samples, classify them into known families, and identify new variants based on their behavioral characteristics and code analysis. This helps security teams stay updated with the latest ransomware trends and develop appropriate defense strategies.

Phishing and Social Engineering Detection:

AI and ML can analyze email and network traffic to identify phishing attempts and social engineering techniques commonly used to deliver ransomware. By examining email content, headers, and sender reputation, these technologies can flag suspicious emails and provide real-time warnings to users. ML algorithms can also learn from historical phishing data to improve detection accuracy and adapt to new phishing techniques.

Incident Response and Recovery:

AI and ML can play a significant role in incident response and recovery processes after a ransomware attack. These technologies can aid in identifying the extent of the attack, prioritizing response actions, and automating certain tasks, such as isolating affected systems, restoring backups, or decrypting files. ML algorithms can also analyze post-incident data to improve future incident response strategies and enhance recovery processes.

User and Entity Behavior Analytics (UEBA):

UEBA leverages AI and ML to monitor and analyze user behavior, detecting anomalies that may indicate compromised accounts or insider threats leading to ransomware attacks. By establishing a baseline of normal user behavior, UEBA can identify suspicious activities, such as unauthorized access attempts or unusual data transfer activities. Early detection of compromised accounts can help prevent ransomware attacks from spreading and minimize their impact.

Threat Intelligence and Predictive Analysis:

AI and ML algorithms can process large volumes of threat intelligence data from various sources to identify emerging ransomware threats and predict future attack trends. By analyzing historical data, trends, and attacker techniques, these technologies can provide organizations with actionable insights and help them proactively prepare for potential ransomware attacks.

However, it's important to note that AI and ML are not standalone solutions but rather complementary components of a comprehensive ransomware defense strategy. Human expertise, regular updates, continuous monitoring, and integration with existing security tools and processes are crucial for maximizing the effectiveness of AI and ML in ransomware defense.

As ransomware attacks become more sophisticated, organizations must leverage AI and ML technologies to augment their defenses and stay ahead of evolving threats. By harnessing the power of these advanced technologies, organizations can enhance their ability to detect, prevent, and respond to ransomware attacks, ultimately safeguarding their data, systems, and reputation.

10.3 Predictive Analytics and Threat Hunting

In the ever-changing landscape of ransomware attacks, organizations need to adopt proactive measures to stay ahead of emerging threats. Predictive analytics and threat hunting are two key strategies that can significantly enhance an organization's ransomware defense capabilities. In this chapter, we will explore the role of predictive analytics and threat hunting in identifying and mitigating ransomware threats.

Predictive Analytics:

Predictive analytics involves the use of advanced algorithms and historical data to forecast potential future events. When applied to ransomware defense, predictive analytics can help organizations anticipate and prevent ransomware attacks before they occur. By analyzing patterns, trends, and indicators of compromise, predictive analytics models can identify early warning signs of ransomware activity. These models can assess various data sources, such as network traffic, system logs, and user behavior, to detect anomalies and generate predictive insights.

Threat Intelligence Integration:

To effectively leverage predictive analytics in ransomware defense, organizations should integrate threat intelligence feeds into their analysis models. Threat intelligence provides valuable information about the latest ransomware variants, attack techniques, and indicators of compromise. By incorporating real-time threat intelligence data into predictive analytics models, organizations can enhance their ability to detect and mitigate ransomware threats. This integration enables organizations to stay informed about the evolving threat landscape and adapt their defense strategies accordingly.

Machine Learning Algorithms:

Machine learning algorithms are an integral part of predictive analytics for ransomware defense. These algorithms can analyze large datasets, learn from historical ransomware attacks, and identify patterns and correlations that may not be apparent to human analysts. By training machine learning models on known ransomware samples and their characteristics, organizations can develop models capable of detecting and classifying new ransomware variants. Machine learning algorithms can also assist in identifying false positives and reducing the number of manual investigations required.

Threat Hunting:

Threat hunting involves proactively searching for threats and indicators of compromise within an organization's environment. This proactive approach goes beyond traditional security measures and allows organizations to actively seek out ransomware threats that may have evaded detection. Threat hunting involves utilizing various techniques, such as log analysis, network monitoring, and behavioral analytics, to identify potential ransomware activities. Skilled threat hunters leverage their knowledge of the organization's infrastructure and the latest attack techniques to uncover hidden threats and take necessary actions to prevent or mitigate potential ransomware attacks.

Collaborative Threat Hunting:

Collaboration among organizations and security communities is becoming increasingly important in the context of threat hunting. By sharing threat intelligence, indicators of compromise, and hunting methodologies, organizations can collectively improve their ability to detect and respond to ransomware threats. Collaborative threat hunting enables organizations to benefit from shared expertise, insights, and detection capabilities. This approach strengthens the overall security posture and helps organizations stay ahead of rapidly evolving ransomware attacks.

Automation and Orchestration:

To effectively conduct predictive analytics and threat hunting at scale, organizations should consider leveraging automation and orchestration tools. These tools can streamline data collection, analysis, and response processes, enabling security teams to focus on higher-level decision-making and proactive threat hunting. Automation can help accelerate the identification and remediation of ransomware threats, reduce response times, and improve overall operational efficiency.

Predictive analytics and threat hunting play crucial roles in proactively identifying and mitigating ransomware threats. By leveraging these strategies, organizations can stay one step ahead of attackers and minimize the potential impact of ransomware attacks. It is essential to invest in the necessary tools, technologies, and skilled personnel to implement predictive analytics and threat hunting effectively.

10.4 Quantum Computing and Its Potential Impact on Ransomware

Quantum computing is a rapidly advancing field that has the potential to revolutionize various industries, including cybersecurity. In this chapter, we will explore the potential impact of quantum computing on ransomware and the implications it may have for organizations' defense strategies.

Quantum Computing Basics:

Quantum computing leverages the principles of quantum mechanics to perform complex computations more efficiently than classical computers. Quantum bits, or qubits, can exist in multiple states simultaneously, allowing quantum computers to handle vast amounts of data and perform calculations at an exponential speed compared to traditional computers.

Breaking Encryption Algorithms:

One of the potential impacts of quantum computing on ransomware is its ability to break commonly used encryption algorithms. Many encryption algorithms currently in use, such as RSA and ECC, rely on the difficulty of factoring large prime numbers or solving the discrete logarithm problem. Quantum computers, with their immense computational power, could potentially solve these problems in a significantly shorter time, rendering current encryption methods vulnerable to attacks.

Cryptographic Solutions for the Post-Quantum Era:

nt of quantum computing necessitates the ent and adoption of new cryptographic solutions resistant to quantum attacks. Post-quantum cryptography focuses on developing encryption algorithms and cryptographic protocols that are secure against attacks by quantum computers. Organizations need to be prepared for this shift and proactively transition to post-quantum cryptographic solutions to ensure the continued security of their data.

Quantum-Safe Encryption and Key Distribution:

Quantum-safe encryption algorithms, also known as quantum-resistant or post-quantum encryption, are designed to withstand attacks from quantum computers. These algorithms are being developed to replace current encryption methods and provide secure communication channels even in the presence of quantum computing capabilities. Additionally, quantum key distribution (QKD) protocols utilize the principles of quantum mechanics to ensure secure key exchange between parties, protecting sensitive data from interception or decryption by quantum computers.

Impact on Ransomware Attacks:

Quantum computing could potentially have a significant impact on the field of ransomware. As quantum computers become more powerful, attackers with access to such computing capabilities could potentially break encryption algorithms used to protect sensitive data. This could lead to the decryption of encrypted files and render ransomware attacks less effective.

Quantum-Resistant Defense Strategies:

To prepare for the era of quantum computing, organizations must adopt quantum-resistant defense strategies. This includes implementing post-quantum encryption algorithms, updating cryptographic protocols, and transitioning to quantum-safe key management systems. By proactively addressing the potential impact of quantum computing on ransomware, organizations can mitigate the risk of data breaches and ensure the confidentiality and integrity of their sensitive information.

Quantum Computing for Ransomware Development:

It is worth considering that while quantum computing may have an impact on the security landscape, it could also be leveraged by malicious actors to develop more sophisticated ransomware. Quantum computing could potentially enable the creation of advanced encryption algorithms that are resistant to classical decryption methods, making it more challenging for defenders to mitigate the impact of ransomware attacks.

Collaborative Efforts and Research:

The development and implementation of quantum-resistant cryptographic solutions require collaborative efforts between academia, industry, and government entities. Ongoing research and collaboration are crucial to ensure the development of robust and standardized post-quantum encryption algorithms and protocols. Organizations should actively participate in industry initiatives and stay updated with the latest advancements in quantum-resistant cryptography to adapt their defense strategies accordingly.

While quantum computing's full potential and timeline for practical implementation are still being explored, organizations should be aware of its potential impact on ransomware and the need to embrace quantum-safe defense strategies. By staying informed, collaborating with experts, and investing in research and development, organizations can prepare themselves to address the challenges and opportunities presented by the era of quantum computing.

In "Ransomware Defense Strategies - Proven Defense Strategies for Today's Threat Landscape," I present a comprehensive guide to protecting against the growing menace of ransomware attacks. Drawing on my extensive experience as a cybersecurity professional, this book equips readers with the knowledge and strategies needed to safeguard their digital assets.

The book begins by introducing readers to the world of ransomware, providing an understanding of its origins, impact, and various types. We explore the anatomy of ransomware attacks, dissecting the stages and common attack vectors used by cybercriminals to infiltrate systems and encrypt critical data.

To fortify our defenses, we delve into assessing security postures. Readers will learn how to conduct a thorough security risk assessment, identify vulnerabilities, and evaluate their readiness to defend against ransomware. Building upon this foundation, we explore strategies for building a resilient infrastructure, including robust backup and disaster recovery plans, network and endpoint security measures, and secure configurations and access controls.

Recognizing the vital role of user awareness and training, we discuss the importance of educating employees about ransomware risks and implementing secure practices for email, web browsing, and file sharing. By fostering a culture of security within organizations, we empower individuals to become active participants in ransomware defense.

Should an incident occur, the book provides a roadmap for effective incident response and recovery. We guide readers through the development of an incident response plan, containment strategies, mitigation techniques, and data recovery methods. By understanding the steps involved in responding to a ransomware attack, readers can minimize the impact and restore operations swiftly.

Moving beyond the basics, we explore advanced defense techniques. This includes leveraging threat intelligence, proactive monitoring, behavior-based detection, and machine learning to stay one step ahead of attackers. We also delve into encryption and data protection mechanisms, as well as the use of deception technologies to deceive and confound ransomware operators.

Recognizing the power of collaboration, we emphasize the importance of information sharing within the industry. By engaging with peers, security communities, and law enforcement agencies, readers can tap into collective knowledge, share threat intelligence, and strengthen their defense strategies.

Compliance with data protection regulations and standards is a critical aspect of any ransomware defense strategy. The book provides insights into relevant compliance considerations, helping readers align their efforts with industry-specific security frameworks.

Finally, we turn our gaze towards the future, exploring emerging trends and technologies in ransomware defense. We discuss the potential impact of artificial intelligence, machine learning, quantum computing, and predictive analytics on the ransomware landscape, enabling readers to prepare for the challenges that lie ahead.

With a focus on practicality and real-world examples, "Ransomware Defense Strategies" empowers readers to take proactive measures in defending against ransomware attacks. By implementing the proven strategies outlined in this book, individuals and organizations can protect their valuable assets and mitigate the risk of falling victim to ransomware.

Together, let's rise to the challenge and safeguard our digital world from the threat of ransomware.

Jack Taylor